Building English Skills

Plum Level

Purple Level

Yellow Level

Blue Level

Orange Level

Green Level

Red Level

Gold Level

Silver Level

Aqua Level

Brown Level

PLUM LEVEL

Pink Level

Kindergarten Level

McDougal, Littell & Company

Evanston, Illinois

New York   Dallas   Sacramento

Author

Gail M. Griffin, Specialist in Elementary Education, Branford, Connecticut

Consultants

Karen Antine, Teacher, East Cleveland City School District, East Cleveland, Ohio

Eve D. Beverly, Ph.D., Educational Consultant and Teacher, Deerfield, Illinois

Elizabeth B. Buenning, Teacher, Community Consolidated School District 15, Palatine, Illinois

Phyllis W. Dole, Language Arts Consultant and Teacher, San Juan Capistrano, California

Pearl Neumann Fox, Teacher, District 109, Deerfield, Illinois

Marion Golding, Teacher, District 109, Deerfield, Illinois

Cathy Zollars, Director of Instruction, Grand Prairie Schools, Grand Prairie, Texas

Acknowledgments Coward, McCann & Geoghegan, Inc.: For an adaptation of the text and three illustrations from *Fiona's Bee* by Beverly Keller, illustrations by Diane Paterson; copyright © 1975 by Beverly Keller; illustrations © 1975 by Diane Paterson. Doubleday & Company, Inc.: For "Vegetables," from *Taxis and Toadstools* by Rachel Field; copyright 1926 by Doubleday & Company, Inc. (Continued on page 202.)

Editorial Director: Joy Littell

Editor: Patricia Opaskar

Assistant Editor: Bernice Rappoport

Design: Image Concepts Ltd.

ISBN: 0-86609-066-5

Contents

Chapter 1 Using Language 1

Sharing Jobs at School   3
Sharing Jobs at Home   5
Getting Help   7
Learning from Others   9

Learning About a Job   11
Writing About a Job   13
Checking Your Skills   14

Chapter 2 Working with Words 15

Words That Rhyme   17
Words That Sound the Same   19
Words That Have Almost the Same
  Meaning   21
Words That Have Opposite
  Meanings   23

Compound Words   25
Contractions   27
Writing About Food   29
Checking Your Skills   30

Chapter 3 Sentences 31

What Is a Sentence?   33
Finding Sentences   34
The Naming Part of a Sentence   35
Finding the Naming Part of a
  Sentence   36
The Telling Part of a Sentence   37
Finding the Telling Part of a
  Sentence   38
Different Kinds of Sentences   39
Finding Statements and
  Questions   40
Writing Statements   41
Writing Questions   43

Commands   45
Finding Statements, Questions,
  and Commands   46
Writing Commands   47
Writing Sentences   48
Exclamations   49
Finding Four Kinds of
  Sentences   50
Writing Exclamations   51
Writing All Four Kinds of
  Sentences   52
Writing About a Game   53
Checking Your Skills   54

Chapter 4   Using a Dictionary   55

Listing Words in ABC Order   57
More About ABC Order   59
Finding the Meaning of a Word   60
Listening for Sounds in Words   61

Finding the Spelling of a
    Word   63
Writing About Nature   65
Checking Your Skills   66

Chapter 5   Nouns   67

Finding and Using Nouns   69
One and More than One   71
Nouns That Name One or More
    than One   73
Nouns That Change Their Forms   74
Proper Nouns   75
Titles   76

More About Proper Nouns   77
Names of Days   79
Writing Names of Days   80
Names of Months   81
Writing Dates   82
Writing About a Place   83
Checking Your Skills   84

Chapter 6   Writing Letters   85

Writing an Invitation   87
Writing a Thank-You Letter   89
Addressing an Envelope   91
Studying a Friendly Letter   93

Writing the Message   94
Writing a Friendly Letter   95
Checking Your Skills   96

Chapter 7   Verbs   97

Finding and Using Verbs   99
More About Verbs   101
Verbs with One or More than
    One   103
Forms of **Be**   105
Forms of **Have**   106
Now and in the Past   107

Using **Be** To Tell About the
    Past   109
Using **Have** To Tell About the
    Past   111
More About the Past   113
Writing About Machines   115
Checking Your Skills   116

Chapter 8   Writing Book Reports   117

Learning About Books   119
What Is the Book About?   121
Thinking About the Story   123
Thinking More About the Story   125

Writing a Book Report   127
Giving a Book Report   129
Checking Your Skills   130

Chapter 9   Pronouns   131

Using I and Me   133
Using We and Us   135
Pronouns as the Naming Part of
    the Sentence   137

Pronouns in Other Parts of the
    Sentence   138
Writing About a Hero   139
Checking Your Skills   140

Chapter 10   Writing a Story   141

Ideas That Go Together   143
Telling Things in Order   145
Starting Your Story   147
Writing Your Story   149

Ending Your Story   150
Making Your Story Better   151
Checking Your Skills   152

Chapter 11   Words That Describe   153

Words That Tell How Many   155
Words That Tell What Color   156
Words That Tell About the Look
    of a Thing   157
Words That Tell the Feel
    of a Thing   158
Words That Tell About Sound
    or Smell   159
Words That Tell About
    Taste   160

Words That Compare Two
    Things   161
Words That Compare Three or
    More Things   162
Words That Tell About
    Actions   163
Writing About a Special
    Thing   165
Checking Your Skills   166

Chapter 12 Writing a Description 167

Planning How To Describe
    Something 169
Reading a Description 171

Writing a Description 172
Making Your Work Better 173
Checking Your Skills 174

Handbook Using Capital Letters and Punctuation Marks 175

Using Capital Letters for Special
    Words 176
Using Capital Letters for First
    Words 177
Using the Period 178

Using the Question Mark and
    Exclamation Point 179
Using the Comma 180
Using the Apostrophe 181
Writing Titles of Books 182

Dictionary 183

Stories for Good Listening 195

To be read by the teacher at the beginning of the chapters.

Index 199

Chapter 1
Using Language

● **Listen as your teacher reads the story.**

Which jobs do you know about?

Which jobs would you like to know about?

Teacher: You will find a poem or story to introduce each chapter on pages 195 to 198 of this text.

A Talk about the jobs in this list.
Write the jobs you can do now.

Learn in school   Fix holes in the road

Teach in school   Do homework

Fight fires   Build houses

Drive a bus   Set a table

Follow safety rules   Sell things in a store

B You must speak and listen to learn in school.
You must speak and listen to teach in school.
Think about the jobs on the list.
Which of those jobs need speaking and listening?
List five of the jobs that use language.

C Draw a picture
    of yourself.
Show a job you
    can do now.

2

Sharing Jobs at School

Ⓐ Talk about each part of the picture.
How are the children working with the grown-ups?

Ⓑ Tell how these workers use language in their jobs.

1. Librarian	2. Teacher	3. Custodian
4. Secretary	5. Doctor	6. Cook

A Write the things you do at school now.
Draw a line under the one you like best.

1. Read

2. Keep the room clean

3. Help children across streets

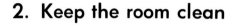

4. Do arithmetic

5. Work at my seat

6. Paint

7. Carry things

8. Help the teacher

B When you grow up, you might like to work at a school.
What job would you like? Write the answer.
Talk about your answer. Tell why you chose it.

4

Sharing Jobs at Home

A Talk about the pictures.
How are these families making their homes
good places to live in?

B Tell which pictures show jobs you have done.

A Write a list of jobs you do at home.

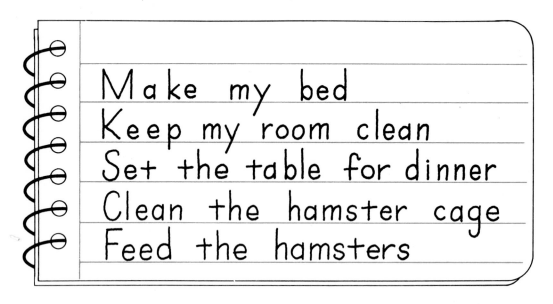

Make my bed
Keep my room clean
Set the table for dinner
Clean the hamster cage
Feed the hamsters

B Here are four workers who help us have
the things we need at home.
Tell how these workers use language in their jobs.

| Clerk | Factory Worker | Plumber | Mover |

C When you grow up, your job might make homes
good places to live in.
What job would you like? Write your answer.
Talk about your answer. Tell why you chose it.

6

Getting Help

A Is it important to say these things? Write Yes or No.

1. There is a fire in the building next to 205 Hill Street.

2. My sister saw the fire first.

3. My friend fell off his bike. His leg hurts.

4. We are near the corner of Main and Oak Streets.

B These four workers help keep us safe and healthy. Tell how they use language in their jobs.

Paramedic   **Firefighter**   **Dentist**   **Police Officer**

A Talk about the picture.
What should the boy do?
What should he say?

B Copy this list.
Fill in the phone numbers.
Keep your list near the phone at home.

> **Emergency Phone Numbers**
>
> **Fire**
> **Police**
> **Doctor**
> **Neighbor**
> **Other**

Learning from Others

These children are using language to get help.
● Write which worker can help each child.

I'm lost. Where should I go?

1. ___

I just got a puppy. Where can I get a book about dogs?

2. ___

I don't feel well. What should I do?

Will the weather be good for a picnic tomorrow?

3. ___   4. ___

Librarian

Doctor

Officer

Forecaster

9

A Take turns in class. Talk about each problem below.
Tell what you would say. Show what you would do.

I'm new at school. Where is the office?

I want to play Simon Says, but I don't know how.

When you talk to the class, follow these rules.
Think about what you are saying.
Talk loudly enough for everyone to hear.

B These workers tell us about new things.
Tell why it is important for them to use language well.

Writer   **Reporter**   **Sports Announcer**   **Salesperson**

C When you grow up, you may like one of these jobs.
What job would you like? Tell why you chose it.

Learning About a Job

● Do these things.
1. Talk with a grown-up at home or at school.
2. Ask the grown-up to help with these questions.
3. When you have answers to the questions,
   share them with your class.
   Tell the class what you learned.

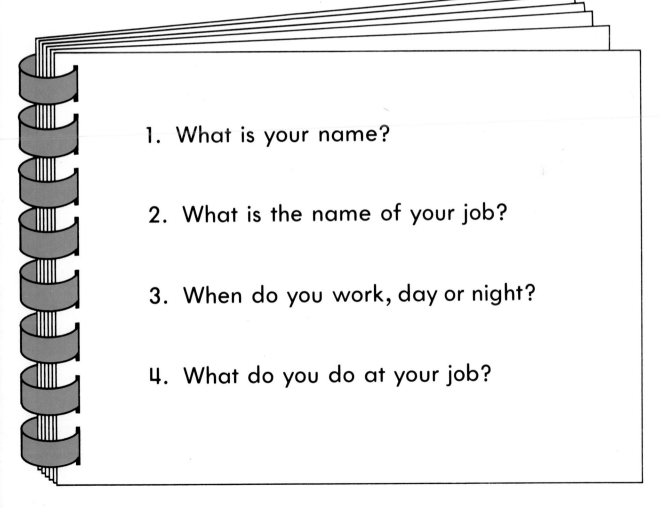

1. What is your name?

2. What is the name of your job?

3. When do you work, day or night?

4. What do you do at your job?

5. Do you use any special tools or machines?

6. How do they help do the job?

7. Do you wear special clothes?

8. Why do you need the special clothes?

9. How did you learn your job?

10. What do you like best about your job?

Writing About a Job

Use drawing paper.

A Draw what you want to be when you grow up.
You may choose one of the jobs on this page.
You may choose a different job.

B Think of an ending for each sentence below.
Write the sentences on writing paper.
Talk about your sentences.

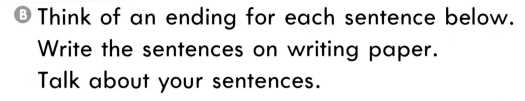

1. When I grow up, I want to be a _____ .

2. I would like to do that because _____ .

13

Checking Your Skills

Ⓐ The boy wants to help the firefighters.
Is it important for him to say these things?
Write Yes or No.

1. There's a fire in a trash can.
2. The fire is in front of 105 North Street.
3. I was walking my dog.

Ⓑ Do these jobs use language? Write Yes or No.

1. Teacher
2. Police officer
3. Doctor

4. Reporter
5. Librarian
6. Sales person

Chapter 2 **Working with Words**

● Listen as your teacher reads the story.

Talk about the story.

How do the soldiers use words to trick
   the people in the town?

15

Ⓐ Listen as your teacher reads this poem.

Vegetables

Some beans have strings to tie them on.
And, what is still more queer,
Ripe corn is nothing more or less
Than one enormous ear!

But when potatoes all have eyes,
Why is it they should be
Put in the ground and covered up—
Where it's too dark to see?

—Rachel Field

Ⓑ Talk about the poem.
How does it use words to make you laugh?

Ⓒ Write each word for two pictures.

eyes   ear   strings

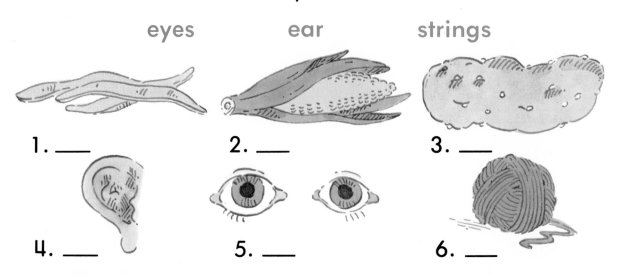

1. ___   2. ___   3. ___

4. ___   5. ___   6. ___

Words That Rhyme

Some words rhyme.
They end with the same sounds.
They do not always end with the same letters.

I eat my peas with honey.
I've done it all my life.
It makes them taste quite funny,
But it keeps them on my knife.

● Write the words that rhyme with money.
Then write the words that rhyme with wife.

Ⓐ In each line, write which pictures rhyme.

1. A.  B.  C.  D.

2. A.   B.  C.  D.

Ⓑ In each line, write which words rhyme.

1.   bean   queen   green   plate

2.   carry   bunny   money   honey

Ⓒ Write each blue word. Write a word that rhymes with it.

Jack Spratt
Could eat no ____ .
His wife could eat no lean.
And so between them both you see,
They licked the plate quite ____ .

Words That Sound the Same

Some words may sound the same.
They may not mean the same thing.

Meet my father.
He is cooking meat.

I ate
eight cupcakes.

● Choose the correct word for each sentence. Write it.

1. no, know   I have ___ pencil.
2. here, hear   Did you ___ the story?
3. to, too, two   We ate ___ apples.
4. read, red   Have you ___ this book?
5. blew, blue   She wore a ___ shirt.

19

Some words that are spelled the same do not mean the same thing.

The baby gave the ball a roll.

Mom gave me a roll for breakfast.

● Write the sentence that matches the picture.

1. That tree has brown bark.

   Does your dog bark at trucks?

2. I sit in the first row.

   Can you row the boat?

3. The runners train.

   I rode the train.

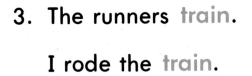

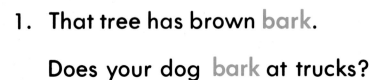

20

Words That Have Almost the Same Meaning

Two words may have almost the same meaning.

● Talk about the words in the picture.
Write the words that have almost the same meaning.

1. _____ flapjack
2. _____ cook
3. _____ pot
4. _____ plate
5. _____ cup
6. _____ hat

A Which word matches? Write the letter.

1. rush __E__

2. happy ____

3. beautiful ____

4. cart ____

5. shut ____

A. glad

B. close

C. wagon

D. pretty

E. hurry

B Write a word that has almost the same meaning.

big   forest   sad   small   thin

1. skinny ____
2. large ____
3. unhappy ____
4. little ____
5. woods ____

22

Words That Have Opposite Meanings

These pairs of words have opposite meanings.

on — off   hot — cold   in — out   tall — short

Ⓐ Talk about the picture.

Can you use any other opposites to tell about it?

Ⓑ Write the opposite of each word.

1. funny _____   bad

2. good _____   low

3. near _____   far

4. high _____   tall

5. short _____   sad

A Find the opposites that fit in the story.
Write the opposites.

dry   day   down   in   swim   under

What would happen in an opposite world?

1. Plants would grow _____ , not up.

2. Planes would fly _____ the land, not over.

3. People would sleep all_____ , not at night.

4. The sea would be _____ , not wet.

B Write the opposites.

sad   old   in   cry   come   late

1. _____ out   4. _____ happy

2. _____ go   5. _____ laugh

3. _____ early   6. _____ new

Compound Words

buttermilk

pancakes

cookbook

Each of these words has two little words in it.

pancake = pan + cake   cookbook = cook + book

A word made of two little words is a compound word.

● Write the two little words in each compound word.

1. buttermilk = ____ + ____

2. oatmeal = ____ + ____

3. applesauce = ____ + ____

4. gingerbread = ____ + ____

Many long words are made of two little words.
Think of how you spell each of the two little words.
Then you can spell the compound word.

● Put the two blue words together
    to make one compound word.
Write the compound word.

1. Meat made into a ball is a ____.

2. Corn that goes pop is ____.

3. A ____ is a cake with fruit in it.

4. A cloth that covers a table is a ____.

5. A cake as small as a cup is a ____.

6. To make a ____ , you turn one half
    of the crust over the other half.

26

Contractions

See how two words become one word.

The cake is not rising.   The cake isn't rising.
It will not taste good.   It won't taste good.
I am not hungry.   I'm not hungry.

The blue words are contractions.

A contraction is a word that puts together two words.

Every contraction has an apostrophe.   '
The apostrophe shows that the letters have been left out.

Which contraction puts together each pair of words?
● Write the contraction.

1. is not <u>isn't</u>   haven't

2. could not _____   weren't

3. have not _____   won't

4. were not _____   isn't

5. will not _____   it's

6. it is _____   couldn't

Here are some contractions that you should know.
See where the apostrophe belongs.

A Think of the letters that are left out.

I'm	I am	isn't	is not
we're	we are	aren't	are not
you're	you are	doesn't	does not
he's	he is	don't	do not
she's	she is	won't	will not
it's	it is	hasn't	has not
they're	they are	haven't	have not
we'll	we will	can't	can not

B Write each sentence.
Fill in the correct contraction.

1. have not   We ___ eaten yet.
2. is not   Mom ___ home
3. She is   ___ still at her job.
4. We are   ___ getting dinner ready.
5. can not   Dad ___ find any flour.
6. We will   ___ cook a good meal.

28

Writing About Food

A Use drawing paper. Draw something you like to eat.

B Use writing paper.

Finish each of these sentences about the food.

One of my favorite foods is ____.

I like it because ____.

29

Checking Your Skills

A Write the words that rhyme.

A	B
1. rice ___	steam
2. cream ___	able
3. table ___	ice

B Write the red words on your paper.
Then write these words in the right places.

quick   still   start   stop   loud   slow

	same meaning	opposite meaning
1. begin	___	___
2. fast	___	___
3. quiet	___	___

C Write the correct contraction.

hasn't   they're   haven't   it's   he's   can't

1. have not ___   3. they are ___
2. it is ___   4. can not ___

30

Chapter 3 Sentences

● Listen as your teacher reads the story.
Talk about the picture.
Which games have you played?

You use words to tell ideas. You put words in order.

These words are out of order. They do not tell an idea.

followed Peter Janie.

These words are in order.

Peter followed Janie.
Janie followed Peter.

The order is different in each group.
The idea is different in each group.

● Which picture matches each sentence? Write the letter.

A   B

1. Peter followed Janie.

2. Janie followed Peter.

3. Ann tagged Ken.

4. Ken tagged Ann.

5. Lee will catch Mary.

6. Mary will catch Lee.

What Is a Sentence?

A sentence is a group of words.
The words are in order.
The words tell a complete idea.

These words are a sentence. They tell an idea.

The children play a game.

These words are not a sentence.
They do not tell an idea.

The children.

● Are these word groups sentences? Write **Yes** or **No**.

1. On the floor.	1. <u>No</u>
2. Everyone sat on the floor.	2. ___
3. All the red markers.	3. ___
4. All the red markers are in the box.	4. ___
5. The children had fun.	5. ___

Finding Sentences

> **A** sentence **is a group of words that tells a complete idea.**

Example   Many people play checkers.

● Tell which groups are sentences.
Write Yes or No.

1. Kay and Bill like checkers.   1. _Yes_

2. They play together.   2. ____

3. Wins many games.   3. ____

4. Kay takes the red checkers.   4. ____

5. She likes red better.   5. ____

6. Tomorrow at Bill's house.   6. ____

7. Bill was careful.   7. ____

8. All of the black checkers.   8. ____

9. With her king.   9. ____

10. Bill won.   10. ____

The Naming Part of a Sentence

A sentence names who or what does something.

A Read this sentence.
The words in blue name who does something.

Some children skate well.

The blue words are the naming part of the sentence.
Another name for naming part is subject.

The girls   The dogs   The boys

B Write these sentences. Fill in the naming parts.
Use the names for the pictures above.
Some sentences may have two correct naming parts.

1. ___ are first.

2. ___ are pets.

3. ___ wear skates.

4. ___ are talking.

5. ___ can go fast.

35

Finding the Naming Part of a Sentence

Every sentence has a naming part, or subject. This part names who or what does something.

Example   Many of my friends have pets.

● Write the naming part of each sentence below.

1. All of us like our pets.
2. Animals can be friendly.
3. Kim and her friends held a pet show.
4. Bobby brought his goldfish.
5. His dog came, too.
6. Three cats wore colorful ribbons.
7. A green and yellow parrot talked to us.
8. Kim's turtle crawled under a bush.
9. Many neighbors came to the show.
10. Everyone had a good time.

The Telling Part of a Sentence

> **A sentence tells what a person or thing does.**

A Read this sentence.
The words in blue tell what Lucia does.

    Lucia plays with balls.

The blue words are the telling part
    of the sentence.
Another name for telling part is predicate.

B Write these sentences. Fill in the telling parts.
Choose words from the purple box.

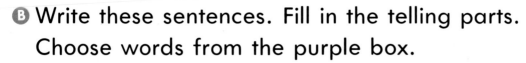

runs.	orange and pink.
jumps rope.	lives near me.
shoes.	has black hair.
plays outside.	

1. Lucia ___.

2. Lucia ___.

3. Lucia ___.

4. Lucia ___.

5. Lucia ___.

Finding the Telling Part of a Sentence

> **Every sentence has a** telling part, **or** predicate.
> **This part tells what the person or thing does.**

Example   Ben <u>can swim under the water.</u>

● Write each sentence below.
Circle the naming part.
Draw a line under the telling part.

1. Judy goes to the pool.

   (Judy) <u>goes to the pool.</u>

2. Her friends swim there.
3. Jeff brings goggles.
4. Tim and Jean take lessons at the pool.
5. They are learning to swim.
6. Fred dives well.
7. The children swim races.
8. They play at the pool all afternoon.

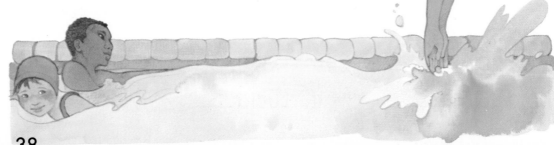

Different Kinds of Sentences

Different sentences do different jobs.
Some sentences tell something.

The children played baseball.

Some sentences ask something.

Who was there?

● What job does each sentence do? Write tell or ask.

1. Ann threw the ball.
2. Is it a strike?
3. Sandy was catcher.

4. Tom had the bat.
5. Did he hit the ball?
6. Who will win?

A sentence that tells something is a statement.
A sentence that asks something is a question.

Finding Statements and Questions

> A sentence that tells something is a statement.
> A sentence that asks something is a question.

● Write what kind each sentence is.

statement   My father plays softball.
question   When does he play?

1. We are going to the ball park.   1. <u>statement</u>

2. Do you want to go, too?   2. _____

3. What teams will play?   3. _____

4. The game will be exciting.   4. _____

5. I went to a game last month.   5. _____

6. Two batters hit home runs.   6. _____

7. What was the score?   7. _____

8. Are you ready?   8. _____

9. You should take sun glasses.   9. _____

10. Where is the ball park?   10. _____

Writing Statements

Ⓐ Find the first letter of each statement.
Tell what kind of letter is used.

1. My friend and I will
play hopscotch.

2. We need a flat place.

Ⓑ Find the mark at the end
of each statement.
Tell what that mark looks like.

> **Every sentence begins with a capital letter.**
> **A statement ends with a period.**
> **A period looks like this.** •

Ⓒ Write each of these sentences correctly.

1. my friend has some chalk

2. she will draw the boxes

3. the game will start now

4. you can go first

5. it is my turn now

**Every sentence begins with a capital letter.
A statement ends with a period.**

Example   In summer we play outside.

Three of these statements are written correctly.
● Find the statements that are not written correctly.
Write those statements only on writing paper.
Begin and end each statement correctly.

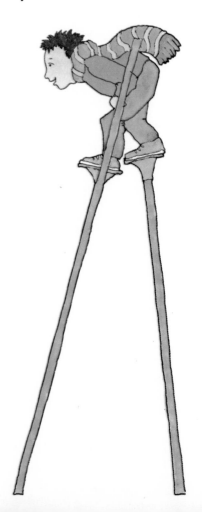

1. Some children jumped rope.

2. Kay had the first turn

3. the rope moved quickly

4. Two boys turned the rope.

5. that girl never misses

6. Some children can walk on stilts.

7. my brother uses stilts

8. He can walk fast

Writing Questions

A Write the first letter of each question.
Copy the mark at the end.
Tell what the end mark looks like.

1. Is this your kite?

2. Did you make it?

> A question ends with a question mark.
> A question mark looks like this.   ?

B Write each of these questions.
Use the right first word. Put a question mark at the end.

1. (is, Is) _____ the wind strong _

2. (Will, will) _____ the kite go up _

3. (do, Do) _____ we need more string _

4. (How, how) _____ did it get into the tree _

5. (Can, can) _____ we get the kite down _

Every sentence begins with a capital letter.
A question ends with a question mark.

lettuce   chair   a sunburned zebra

a needle   corn   a yardstick

● Write each question below on a writing paper.
Begin and end each question correctly.
Then find the answer in the pictures above.
Write the answer after the question.

Sample   what has ears but cannot hear

Answer   What has ears but cannot hear? corn

1. what has three feet but cannot walk
2. what has one eye but cannot see
3. what is black and white and red all over
4. what has a head but cannot think
5. what has four legs but cannot run

Commands

Some sentences tell someone to do something.

"Swing hard."   "Try again."

"Hit the ball."

> **A sentence that tells someone to do something is a command.**

Example   Take your turn next.

In every command, the naming part is You.
Most of the time, you do not say or write the word You.

● Write each of these commands the usual way.
Do not write the naming part.

1. You catch the ball.   1. <u>Catch the ball.</u>

2. You bring your bat.   2. _____

3. You run fast.   3. _____

45

Finding Statements, Questions, and Commands

A statement is a sentence that tells something.
A question is a sentence that asks something.
A command is a sentence that tells someone
    to do something.

● Write which kind each sentence is.

statement   Today the sun is out.
question   Do you want to play?
command   Come to my house.

1. It rained last night.   1. _____
2. Is the ground still wet?   2. _____
3. It is not muddy.   3. _____
4. Bring your Frisbee.   4. _____
5. Who wants to play?   5. _____
6. Pick me.   6. _____
7. Are we ready?   7. _____
8. Throw the Frisbee.   8. _____
9. I must go home now.   9. _____
10. Come again tomorrow.   10. _____

Writing Commands

A Write the first letter of each command.
Copy the end mark. Tell what it looks like.

1. Let Tom come over.

2. Hold tight.

3. Keep the line strong.

4. Don't let go.

> **Every sentence begins with a capital letter.
> A command ends with a period.**

B Find the commands that are not written correctly.
Write them correctly.

1. let me play

2. Tell me the rules.

3. Take another turn.

4. come back tomorrow.

5. Bring your basketball.

6. Don't be late

Writing Sentences

> Every sentence begins with a capital letter.
> A statement or a command ends with a period.
> A question ends with a question mark.

● Write each sentence correctly.

1. (Have, have) _____ you ever played dodgeball _

2. (you, You) _____ need many players _

3. (get, Get) _____ a big ball _

4. (Form, form) _____ a circle _

5. (One, one) _____ player stands in the middle _

6. (throw, Throw) _____ the ball at that player _

7. (Do, do) _____ you want to play _

48

Exclamations

Some sentences show strong feeling.

What a game that was!

We won!

We lost!

A sentence that shows strong feeling is an exclamation.

● Read each sentence Does it show strong feeling? Write Yes or No.

1. That game was so much fun!   1. <u>Yes</u>

2. We played in the field.   2. ___

3. How hot it was!   3. ___

4. I never ran so fast before!   4. ___

5. It was a long game.   5. ___

6. What a good time I had!   6. ___

49

Finding Four Kinds of Sentences

> A statement is a sentence that tells something.
> A question is a sentence that asks something.
> A command is a sentence that tells someone
>   to do something.
> An exclamation is a sentence that shows
>   strong feeling.

● Read each sentence. Write which kind it is.

statement	Christy moved to a new home.
question	Were the neighbor children friendly?
command	Come and play with us.
exclamation	How big the playground is!

1. Have you played before?   1. ____

2. Stand near me.   2. ____

3. Do you know the rules?   3. ____

4. What a catch that was!   3. ____

5. The sun is in my eyes.   5. ____

6. Jump for the ball!   6. ____

7. Don't step in the puddle.   7. ____

8. Everybody played well.   8. ____

Writing Exclamations

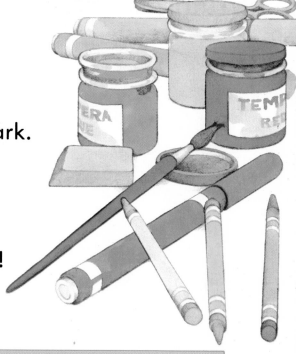

Ⓐ Copy the exclamations below.
Circle the first letter of each.
Draw a line under the end mark.
Tell what the mark looks like.

1. How pretty your picture is!

2. What strong colors you use!

3. Painting pictures is fun!

> **An exclamation ends with an** exclamation point.
> **An exclamation point looks like this.**   !

Ⓑ Write these exclamations correctly.
Use the correct first word in each sentence.
Put an exclamation point at the end.

      what   show   how   you

1. ___ funny animals you draw _
2. ___ work so quickly _
3. ___ big that paper is _
4. ___ me how to draw that _

Writing All Four Kinds of Sentences

Every sentence begins with a capital letter.

A statement or a command ends with a period.
A question ends with a question mark.
An exclamation ends with an exclamation point.

● Write the sentences below.
Begin and end each sentence correctly.

1. (Let's, let's)   _____ have a parade _
2. (can, Can)   _____ we use our bikes _
3. (put, Put)   _____ colored paper on the bikes _
4. (How, how)   _____ bright that looks _
5. (will, Will)   _____ everybody cheer _
6. (How, how)   _____ noisy that would be _

52

Writing About a Game

Use drawing paper.

A Draw an outdoor game you like.

Use writing paper.

B Write two or three sentences about the game.
Tell what it is called. Tell why you like it.

Checking Your Skills

A Write each sentence below.
Fill in the missing part.
Use these words.

<table>
<tr><td>get in a circle</td><td>Works hard</td></tr>
<tr><td>my jacks and ball</td><td>Many children</td></tr>
</table>

1. _____ play dodgeball.

2. All the players _____ .

B Read each of the sentences.
Then write the sentence correctly.
On the line after the sentence, write which kind it is.

statement   question   command   exclamation

1. we will jump rope _____

2. who will jump first _____

3. how high you jump _____

4. please turn the rope _____

54

Chapter 4 Using a Dictionary

Listen as your teacher reads the story.
Are any of the words new to you?

Sometimes you hear a new word.
You don't know what it means.
You want to find out what it means.

Sometimes you want to write a word,
but you don't know how to spell it.
You want to find out how to spell it.

Where do you look?

A dictionary lists words.
It shows how to spell each word.
It tells what each word means.

The words are in groups.
The words in each group begin
    with the same letter.

The groups are in ABC order.
If you know the alphabet, you can use a dictionary.

● Fill in the missing letters. Write the alphabet.

a b _ d _ _ _ h _ j _ _ m _

_ _ q _ _ _ u v _ _ _ z

Listing Words in ABC Order

Each group below is in ABC order.

1	2	3
animal	rock	plant
beach	seaweed	sand
crab	tide	wave

Each group below should list three words in ABC order.
● Write each group. Fill in the missing word.
Use beach, fish, or water.

1	2	3
bird	____	pail
____	clam	tower
shell	snail	____

● Write each group of words
in ABC order.

1
cat
bee
ant

2
mouse
frog
owl

3
pig
squirrel
dog

More About ABC Order

Each group is in ABC order.

1	2	3
flash	thunder	wave
lightning	tide	weather
loud	tornado	wind

● Write each group in ABC order.

1

shower

rain

storm

2

under

umbrella

up

3

coat

cold

cap

Finding the Meaning of a Word

You may read a word that you do not understand.
You can use a dictionary to find its meaning.
You will use ABC order to find the word there.

● Use the Dictionary that begins on page 183.
Find each of these words in the Dictionary.
Write the number of the page where the meaning of the
     word is given.
Then write the meaning of the word.

1. farm   Page ____   Meaning ____

2. garden   Page ____   Meaning ____

3. forest   Page ____   Meaning ____

4. animal   Page ____   Meaning ____

Listening for Sounds in Words

A Which things in each line begin with the same sound?
Write the letters of the pictures.

1. A.   B.   C.   D.

2. A.   B.   C.   D.

3. A.   B.   C.   D.

Often you can think of the beginning letter of a
    word because of its sound.

B Think of the beginning letters of the words
    pictured above. Write the sentences.

1. In row 1, three words begin with ____ .
2. In row 2, three words begin with ____ .
3. In row 3, three words begin with ____ .
4. In row 3, the other word begins with ____ .

A Say the word that names each picture below.
Listen for the beginning sound of each word.
Think of the beginning letter of each word.
On your paper, write the first letter.

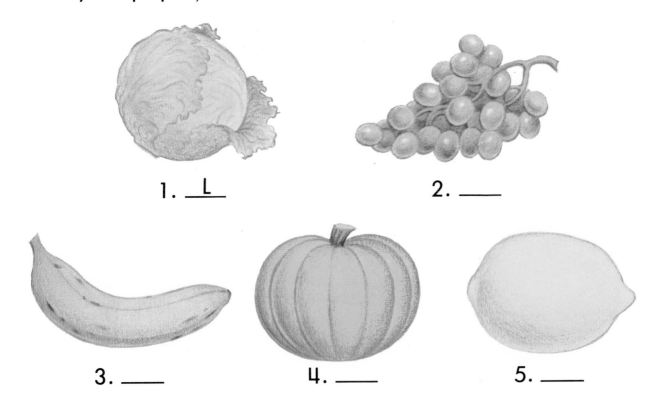

1. __L__   2. ____

3. ____   4. ____   5. ____

B Think of the first two letters of each word above.
Write the letters.

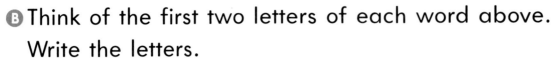

1. ____   2. ____   3. ____   4. ____   5. ____

C Now use the Dictionary beginning on page 183.
Write the page where you find each word.

1. ____   2. ____   3. ____   4. ____   5. ____

Finding the Spelling of a Word

Ⓐ Read each of these words.
Listen for the beginning sounds.

1. giant—juice
2. kite—cat
3. circus—serve

4. fun—phone
5. write—right
6. zebra—xylophone

Different letters can stand for the same sound.
Sometimes you can hear the sound, but you
    will think of the wrong letter.
If a word is not in the Dictionary in the first place
    you look, keep trying.
Look under other letters that stand for
    the same sound.

Ⓑ Use the Dictionary that begins on page 183.
Find each pictured word.
Write the word and the page it is on.

1. ___   2. ___   3. ___

● Write the answers to these riddles.
Find the answers in the Dictionary that begins
    on page 183.
Write the number of the Dictionary page
    where you found the answer.

Animals

1. I have a long, bushy tail. I like to eat
   nuts. I climb trees and run fast. _____ Page _____

2. I have many legs. I can change into a butterfly.
   _____ Page _____

3. I have four legs, a long tail, and sharp
   teeth. I live in or next to rivers. _____ Page _____

4. I am the biggest animal on four feet. ___ Page ___

People

5. I work in a circus. I make people laugh. ___ Page ___

Writing About Nature

Think of your favorite time of year.
Think about the weather and what the plants
    are like then. Think about what the animals do.

Use drawing paper.
Ⓐ Show your favorite time of year.

Use writing paper.
Ⓑ Write two or more sentences about your favorite
    time of year. Your Dictionary will help you to
    spell every word correctly.

Checking Your Skills

Ⓐ Write each group in ABC order.

1	2
grass	sun
tree	snow
flower	sleet

Ⓑ Find the answers to these questions.

The answers are in the Dictionary that begins on
  page 183.

Write each answer.

Spell it correctly.

Then write the number of the Dictionary page
  where you found the answer.

1. I put out fires in homes. ____, Page ____

2. I am in the army. ____, Page ____

Chapter 5 **Nouns**

● Listen as your teacher reads the story.
Try to remember names of people, places,
and things.

A Talk about the story.
Tell some of the names you heard.

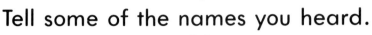

A word that names a person or a
place or a thing is a noun.

Examples friend city bridge

B Write nouns that name what you see
in the picture.
Find the nouns among these words.

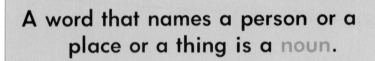

boy   purple   girl   park   and
later   trees   bench   pretty   under

Write names for one place, two persons,
and two things.

Finding and Using Nouns

> **A noun is a word that names a person,**
> **a place, or a thing.**

You can use nouns in the naming part of a sentence.

A little girl with black hair looked at dresses.

● Write each naming part. Circle the noun or nouns.

Sample A little (girl) with black (hair)

1. A boy talked with his mother.
2. Two women had purses.
3. A helpful clerk talked with a man.
4. Clothes hung on the racks.
5. A man with glasses came to the store.

You can use nouns in the telling part of a sentence.

A boy **is carrying three** loaves **of** bread.

● Write the telling part of each sentence.
Then circle the noun or nouns in the telling part.

Sample is carrying three (loaves) of (bread)

1. The little girl wants a roll.
2. Her mother listens to the girl.
3. They will choose a treat.
4. The shelves are full of good things.
5. The baker baked the cookies and bread.

70

One and More than One

A Look at the picture.

Find the nouns that name more than one.

Write the letter at the end of those nouns.

> **Add s to most nouns to make them name more than one.**

Example   one gift   many gifts

B Change each noun to mean more than one. Write it.

1. girl   3. hoop   5. sign

2. boy   4. toy   6. game

● Write a sentence about each prize in the picture.
Tell whether there are two, three, or four of the prize.
Write the noun correctly.

Sample   pig   There are two pigs.

1. duck   1. _____
2. bear   2. _____
3. frog   3. _____
4. dog   4. _____
5. cat   5. _____

72

Nouns That Name One or More than One

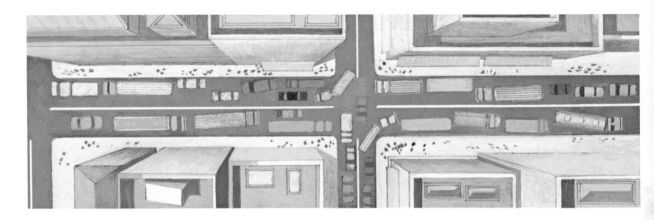

The sentences below use twelve nouns.

● Find all twelve nouns.

Write them on a writing paper.

After each noun, write whether it names one
or more than one thing.

Sample Sentence	Several cars are on the street
Sample Answers	cars—more than one
	street—one

1. The city has many tall buildings.

2. The windows in the stores are pretty.

3. Crowds walk down the streets.

4. My friend took an elevator to the top floor of one
   building.

5. The strong wind shook the windows there.

Nouns That Change Their Forms

Ⓐ These nouns name more than one.
Write each noun next to its form
that names one.

children   men   women

1. man ____
2. woman ____
3. child ____

**Some nouns change their forms
to name more than one.**

Ⓑ Write the sentences below.
Use the correct word in each sentence.

1. A (man, men) looked for shells on the beach.
2. Three (child, children) played in the sand.
3. Two (woman, women) were getting a tan.
4. Another (woman, women) was swimming.
5. A (child, children) waded in the water.
6. Four (man, men) were fishing on the dock.

Proper Nouns

Mr. North

Tim

Liz

Paul

Ms. Lewis

People and some animals have special names.

> **A special name for a person or an animal
>   is a proper noun.**
>
> **Every proper noun begins with a capital letter.**

● Write each proper noun above in the correct place.

Noun	Proper Noun
1. girl	1. ____
2. boy	2. ____
3. man	3. ____
4. woman	4. ____
5. monkey	5. ____

75

Titles

A title is part of a name.

It is part of a proper noun.

Here are some titles that you should know.

Mr.	Use it for any man.
Ms.	Use it for any woman.
Mrs.	Use it for a woman who is married.
Miss	Use it for a woman who is not married.

Begin every title with a capital letter.

Use a period after these titles.

Mr.   Ms.   Mrs.

Do not use a period after this title.

Miss

● Write each of these names.

Begin and end each title correctly.

1. ms brooks

2. miss lane

3. mr kent

4. mrs taylor

5. mr johnson

6. mrs davis

More About Proper Nouns

Ⓐ Many places have special names.
Find five special names for places in the picture.

> **A special name for a place is a proper noun.**
> **A proper noun begins with a capital letter.**

Ⓑ Write the five proper nouns shown in the picture.

1. ___
2. ___
3. ___
4. ___
5. ___

● Write a proper noun for each number.
Use capital letters correctly.

1. Your street
2. Your city or town
3. Your state
4. Your country
5. A place you would like to visit

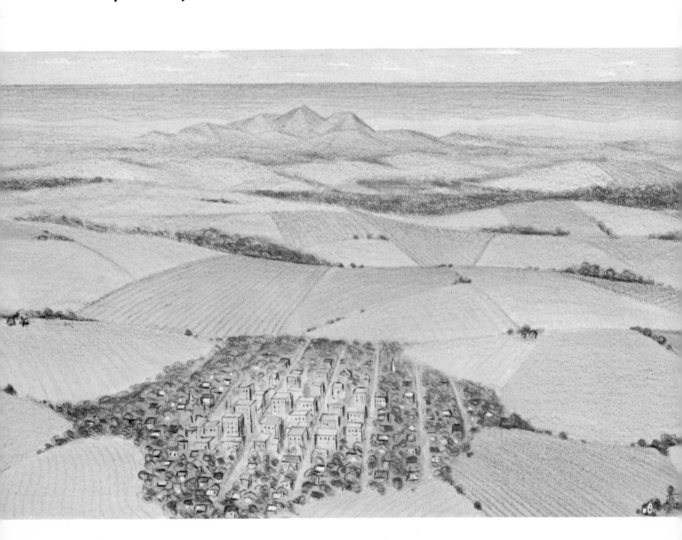

Names of Days

April						
Sunday	Monday	Tuesday	Wednesday	Thursday	Friday	Saturday
	April Fool's Day 1	2	First Day of Passover 3	4	5	6
Easter Sunday 7	8	9	10	11	12	13

Names of days are proper nouns.

Names of holidays are proper nouns.

**A special name for a day is a proper noun.
A proper noun begins with a capital letter.**

Examples   Tuesday   April Fool's Day

● Find the names of days. Write each name correctly.

1. One sunday in May is mother's day.

2. We have thanksgiving on a thursday.

3. Often easter and passover are only a
   few days apart.

Writing Names of Days

● Write these holidays in the order that they happen
    in the year. Look at page 81 for help.
Use capital letters where they are needed.

flag day (June)
independence day (July)
new year's day (January)
memorial day (May)
labor day (September)
veterans day (November)
washington's birthday
    (February)
columbus day (October)

1. <u>New Year's Day</u>
2. ___
3. ___
4. ___
5. ___
6. ___
7. ___
8. ___

Names of Months

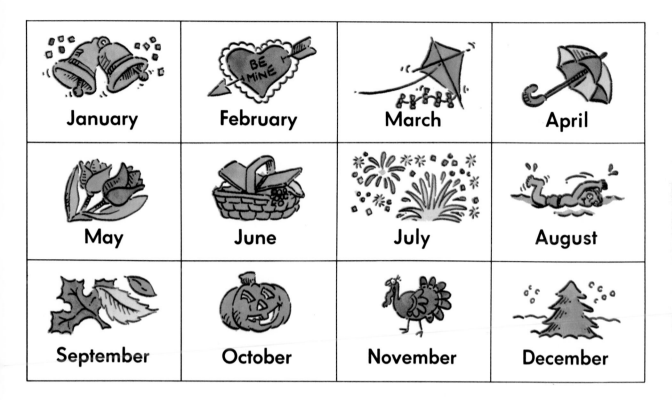

January	February	March	April
May	June	July	August
September	October	November	December

**The name of a month is a proper noun.
A proper noun begins with a capital letter.**

● Write the month when each event below takes place.
Use capital letters correctly.

1. New Year's Day

2. End of the year

3. Halloween

4. Valentine's Day

5. Thanksgiving

6. Your birthday

81

Writing Dates

Here are two ways you can write dates.

1. Write the name of the day with the name of the month and the number of the day.

> Saturday, June 3   Tuesday, April 20

Use a comma after the name of the day. A comma looks like this. ,

2. Write the name of the month and the number of the day with the year.

> June 3, 1983   April 20, 1980

Use a comma after the number of the day.

● Write each date below correctly.

1. september 23 1984   5. wednesday july 18

2. sunday august 6   6. january 8 1976

3. thursday february 2   7. monday march 11

4. october 15 1985   8. november 30 1980

Writing About a Place

Use drawing paper.

Ⓐ Draw a place you have visited.

Use writing paper.

Ⓑ Write two or more sentences about the place.

Use one or more nouns in each sentence.

Checking Your Skills

A Write every noun.

Then circle the nouns that name more than one.

1. My friends are at the station.
2. Their father is buying tickets.
3. Their bags are on a cart.
4. The bus will go through tunnels.
5. The children will enjoy the trip.

B Write the sentences below.

Fill in the missing words.

Use these nouns. Write each proper noun correctly.

monday	new york city
thanksgiving	vacation
ray	jill
mrs taft	mr taft

1. The man at the station is ___.
2. The children are ___ and ___.
3. They will visit ___.
4. Today is ___.
5. The family will eat turkey on ___.

84

Chapter 6 Writing Letters

● Listen as your teacher reads the story.
How were letters useful in the story?
Can you think of other ways letters can be useful?

People write letters for many reasons.

    A. Letters can share news.

    B. Letters can invite someone to do something.

    C. Letters can thank someone.

    D. Letters can cheer up someone who is sick.

● Answer these questions on writing paper.

1. Which kinds of letters have you received?
Write A, B, C, D or None.

2. Which kinds of letters have you sent?
Write A, B, C, D or None.

Most letters have five parts.

    1. The date tells when you wrote the letter.

    2. The greeting tells who is getting the letter.

    3. The message tells what you want to say.

    4. The closing is the way you say goodbye.

    5. The last part is your name.

You will learn more about letters in this chapter.

Writing an Invitation

October 15, 1987

Dear Kathy,

    I am having a Halloween party on Saturday, October 31. It will begin at two o'clock. It will be at my house. I hope you can come.

Your friend,
Steven

● Read the invitation. Answer these questions.

1. When did the writer write the letter? Write the date.
2. Who got the letter? Write the greeting.
3. What does the letter tell about? Write the first three words of the message.
4. Who wrote the letter? Write the closing and the writer's name.

● Help Nancy write an invitation.
Use a sheet of writing paper.
Copy what Nancy wrote.
Fill in the lines.
Tell the day the party
    will be held.
Tell the time.
Tell what kind of party
    it will be.

September 20, 1985

Dear ——— ,

        Can you come to my house for

a —— on ——, ——? It will begin

at —— .

        Your friend,

        Nancy

Writing a Thank-You Letter

March 11, 1984
Dear Aunt Peggy,
Thank you for your gift. I enjoy playing with the yo-yo.
Your niece,
Laura

A Read the letter.

Find the greeting. It tells who is getting the letter.

Find the closing. It is a way of saying goodbye.

Notice where capital letters and commas are used.

> **Begin the** greeting **with a capital letter.**
> **Begin the** closing **with a capital letter.**
>
> **Use a comma in the date.**
> **Use a comma after the greeting.**
> **Use a comma after the closing.**

B Write the greeting and the closing correctly.

Think about a gift you received for a birthday
     or other special day.

Ⓐ Write a thank-you letter.
Copy the parts in the letter below.
Fill in the missing words.
Add commas where they are needed.
Notice where the message begins.
In the message, tell why you liked the gift.

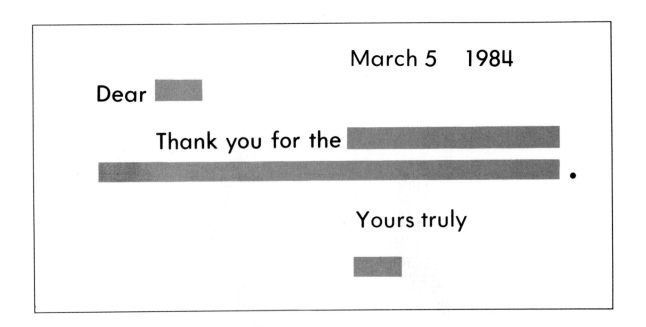

Ⓑ Check your letter.

Did you use capital letters correctly?
Did you use periods correctly?
Did you use commas correctly?

90

Addressing an Envelope

Carol Bank
3839 Frontier Lane
Dallas, Texas 75214

Miss Janet Lee
927 Central Avenue
Albany, New York 12205

A Write one of these answers for each question.

    A. in the top left corner   B. in the middle

1. Where is the sender's name and address?

2. Where is the address of the person who will receive the letter?

B Find the comma in each address.

> **Use a comma in an address.**
> **Put it between a city and a state.**

The numbers after each state name are ZIP codes.

● Draw an envelope on a writing paper.

Fill in the envelope.

Follow the pattern below.

Use your own address in the upper left corner.

That is the return address.

The envelope would be returned to you if it got lost.

Address the envelope to a friend in your school.

Write your friend's name first.

Then write the address of the school.

Make sure that all numbers, including the ZIP
codes, are correct. See that the order is correct.

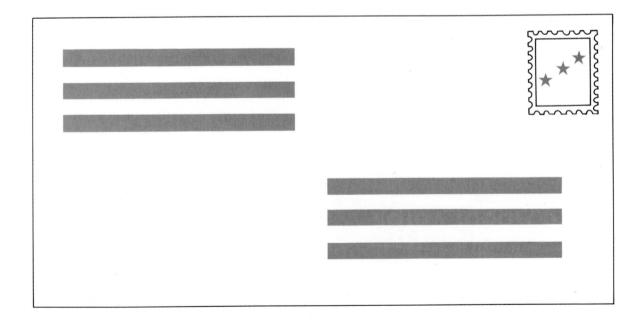

Studying a Friendly Letter

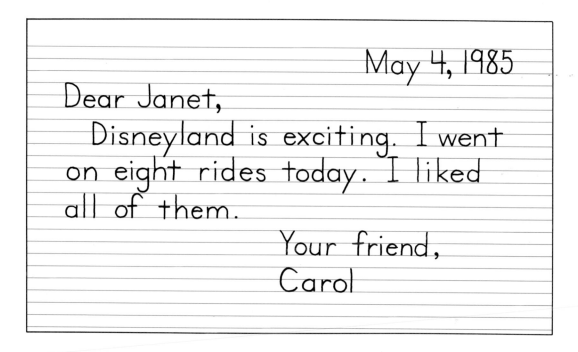

May 4, 1985

Dear Janet,

    Disneyland is exciting. I went on eight rides today. I liked all of them.

            Your friend,
            Carol

● Read the friendly letter above.
Find the answer to each of these questions.
Write the answers on writing paper.

1. On what day did someone write?

2. Who got the letter?

3. What did the writer tell about?

4. How did the writer say goodbye?

5. Who was the writer?

Writing the Message

Before you write a letter, you must know
   two things.

   A. Who will get the letter?

   B. Why are you writing the letter?

● Write the message of a letter.
Do these things.

   1. Choose someone to write to.

   2. Choose a reason for writing.

   3. Think of what you will say.

   4. Write your message.

Writing a Friendly Letter

● Write a complete friendly letter.
Use the message you wrote for page 94,
or write a new message.
Make sure that all five parts are in your letter.
Use capital letters and commas in the right places.

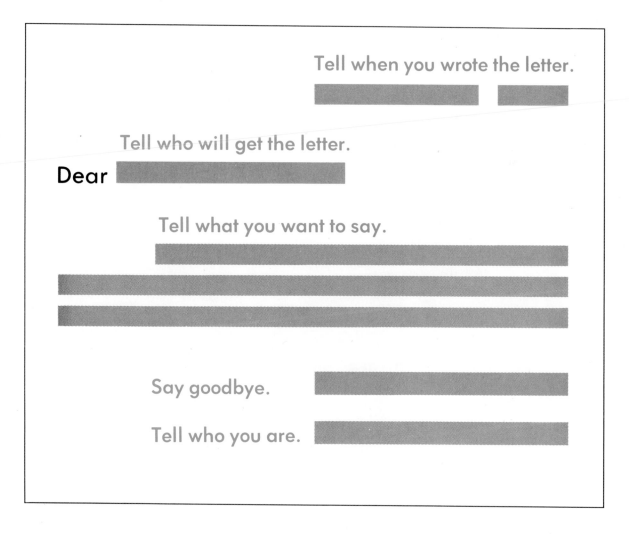

Tell when you wrote the letter.

Tell who will get the letter.

Dear

Tell what you want to say.

Say goodbye.

Tell who you are.

Checking Your Skills

Here are the five parts of a letter.
Some of the parts are written incorrectly.
● Write the letter correctly on your writing paper.
Write each letter part in the right place.
Follow the pattern below.

january 1 1985   Thank you for the funny
your friend   get-well card you sent. I
dear Ellen   laugh each time that I
Paul Donovan   read it.

Chapter 7 **Verbs**

● Listen as your teacher reads the story.
Which words tell what a thing does?
Talk about the story.
Use words that tell what a thing does.

Ⓐ Each of these machines does something.
Match the machine and the doing word.
Write the doing word.

irons   mows   toasts   drills   blends   plays

a toaster   a blender   an iron

1. ___   2. ___   3. ___

a mower   a record player   a drill

4. ___   5. ___   6. ___

Ⓑ Write a sentence about one of the machines.
Use a doing word in the telling part.

Finding and Using Verbs

Some words tell what someone or something does.

Workers **build** houses.   Machines **work** for them.

These words are **verbs**.

Every sentence has a verb.

The verb is the main word in the telling part,
    or predicate, of each sentence.

● Write the predicate in each sentence. Circle the verb.

1. Bulldozers clear the land.   1. (clear) the land
2. Trucks carry dirt away.   2. ___
3. The wind blows the dust and dirt.   3. ___
4. A steam shovel digs the basements.   4. ___
5. A cement mixer brings the cement.   5. ___

Many verbs tell that someone or something does something.

Examples   Sometimes Kim and I **walk** home.
Sometimes we **run**.

● Write the telling part, or predicate, of each sentence. Then circle the verb.

1. We often watch the builders.

   Sample   often (watch) the builders.

2. The workers come each morning.
3. The crane lifts heavy things.
4. Some workers pour concrete.
5. Painters mix their paints.
6. Everyone obeys safety rules.
7. The work stops in the afternoon.
8. The workers go home.

More About Verbs

> Some verbs tell that someone or something
> **has** something.

Examples   Kip **has** a coat. I **have** a jacket.

Ⓐ Write the predicate in each sentence. Circle the verb.

1. Dad has his own truck.
2. The truck has eighteen wheels.
3. The wheels have shiny hubcaps.

1. (has) his own truck
2. ____
3. ____

> Some verbs tell that someone or something
> **is** something.

Examples   Lisa **is** late. We **are** early.

Ⓑ Write the predicate. Circle the verb.

1. My dad is a truck driver.
2. His truck is big.
3. Other truckers are his friends.

1. ____
2. ____
3. ____

101

● Find all the verbs in the sentences below.
Write every verb in the right group.

Two truckers have trouble. Their truck

has a flat tire. They change the tire. A friend

is nearby. The friend helps them. Soon they are

ready to go.

1. Two verbs tell that someone or something
   does something. What are the verbs?

2. Two verbs tell that someone or something
   has something. What are the verbs?

3. Two verbs tell that someone or something
   is something. What are the verbs?

Verbs with One or More than One

A Write the naming part of each sentence.
Then write the verb and circle it.
Tell how the verb changes in
each pair of sentences.

1. One child rides in the car.
2. Two dolls ride on it.

3. The horn makes noise.
4. The wheels make noise.

5. The little girl smiles.
6. Her dolls smile.

> Most verbs that tell about one person
>   or thing end in s.
> Verbs that tell about more than one person
>   or thing have no special ending.

B Write each verb above in the correct group.

One			More than One		
1. __	2. __	3. __	1. __	2. __	3. __

> **Most verbs that tell about one person or thing end in s.**

● Think about the naming part. Write the correct verb.

1. Katy (take, takes) the bus to school.
2. Many children (ride, rides) the bus.
3. The bus (move, moves) down the street.
4. It (stop, stops) for people.
5. Boys and girls (climb, climbs) the steps.
6. Each child (follow, follows) the rules.
7. The driver (sit, sits) in front.
8. Some children (talk, talks) quietly.

Forms of Be

> **The verb be changes in special ways.**
>
> | One | More than One |
> | --- | --- |
> | I am | we are |
> | you are | you are |
> | he is | they are |
> | she is | |
> | it is | |

Examples A tree **is** in our yard.

Many trees **are** on our street.

● Write each sentence below.
Fill in the correct form of be.

1. Our yard ___ large.

2. Flowers ___ in the garden.

3. Dad ___ careful with the yard.

4. I ___ his helper.

5. We ___ proud of our yard.

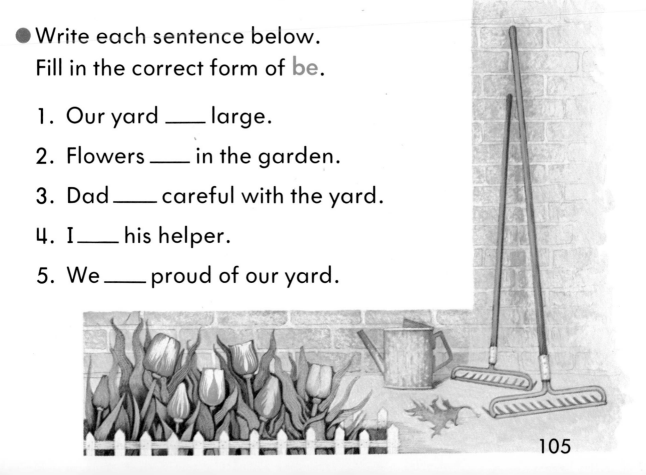

Forms of Have

> **The verb** have **changes in special ways.**
>
> **One**   **More than One**
> I have   we have
> you have   you have
> he has   they have
> she has
> it has

Examples   Rob **has** a vegetable garden.
You **have** a vegetable garden.

● Write the sentences below.
Fill in the correct form of have.

1. The rose bushes ___ flowers.

2. The branches ___ thorns.

3. Mae ___ clippers for cutting branches.

4. She ___ gloves.

5. Now we ___ roses in a vase.

6. The roses ___ a nice smell.

Now and in the Past

A Write these verbs. They tell what happens now.

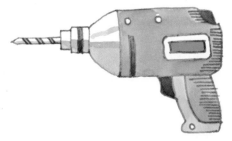

1. This tool drills holes.   2. This one saws wood.

B Write these verbs. They tell
   what happened in the past.
Tell how these verbs are different
   from the verbs above.

1. Mom drilled a hole in the wood.

2. She sawed the wood.

> **Most verbs that tell about the past
> end in ed.**

C Change each verb to tell about the past. Write it.

1. push   2. paint   3. mark   4. count   5. turn

● Find each verb.
Change the verb to tell about the past.
Write your new verb.

1. Everyone works at home.   1. <u>worked</u>

2. Grandma sews torn shirts.   2. ___

3. Jane cleans the rug.   3. ___

4. Mom nails the shelf.   4. ___

5. Bud plays with the baby.   5. ___

6. Dad cooks dinner.   6. ___

7. After dinner we watch TV.   7. ___

8. Machines help us.   8. ___

108

Using Be To Tell About the Past

> ## The verb be changes in special ways.
> am   is   are   was   were

A Write the verbs.

Tell how each verb changes to tell about the past.

Now	In the Past
1. I am in the car.	2. I was in the car.
3. Mom is the driver.	4. Mom was the driver.
5. We are on the road.	6. We were on the road.
7. The hills are far away.	8. The hills were far away.

B Choose the correct form of be. Write the sentence.

1. Tom (was, were) here.
2. Ann (was, were) late.
3. We (were, was) home.
4. I (was, were) cold.
5. They (were, was) hot.

Use **am** or **was** with **I**.
Use **is** or **was** with **one person or thing.**
Use **are** or **were** with **more than one.**
Use **are** or **were** with **you.**

A Write the correct verb.

1. I (am, is, are) on a trip.
2. You (am, is, are) with me.
3. Some trucks (am, is, are) near us.
4. A boat (am, is, are) on a trailer.
5. We (am, is, are) in a traffic jam.

B Make each verb tell about the past.
Write the sentences. Fill in the verbs.

1. I _was_ on a trip.
2. You ____ with me.
3. Some trucks ____ near us.
4. A boat ____ on a trailer.
5. We ____ in a traffic jam.

Using Have To Tell About the Past

> **The verb** have **changes in special ways.**
> has   have   had

A Write the verbs. Tell how the verbs change.

Now

1. I have a friend.
3. He has a sailboat.
5. We have rides on it.

In the Past

2. I had a friend.
4. He had a sailboat.
6. We had rides on it.

B Change each sentence to tell about the past. Write it.

1. Today I have a jacket.
   Last week _____ .
2. Today Kay has sunglasses.
   Yesterday _____ .
3. Now we have a vacation.
   Last year _____ .

> **Use** has **or** had **with one person or thing.**
>
> **Use** have **or** had **with more than one.**
>
> **Use** have **or** had **with I or you.**

Ⓐ Write the correct verb.

1. Many of the boats (has, have) sails.
2. One boat (has, have) a motor.
3. The boats (am, is, are) on the lake.
4. Many people (look, looks) at them.
5. You (has, have) fun on a boat.

Ⓑ Make each verb tell about the past.
Write the sentences. Fill in the verbs.

1. Many of the boats _____ sails.
2. One boat _____ a motor.
3. The boats _____ on the lake.
4. Many people _____ at them.
5. You _____ fun on a boat.

More About the Past

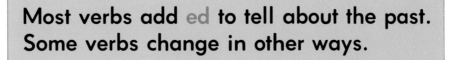

Most verbs add ed to tell about the past. Some verbs change in other ways.

● Find the verbs.
  Match the sentences. Write the letters.

Now	In the Past
1. We see trains.	A. Dad took the train.
2. Dad takes the train.	B. Trains went fast.
3. Trains go fast.	C. Railroads gave jobs to people.
4. They run on tracks.	D. We saw trains.
5. Railroads give jobs to people.	E. They ran on tracks.
6. Railroad workers do many things.	F. Railroad workers did many things.

113

These verbs change in different ways to tell about the past.

Now	Past	Now	Past
do	did	run	ran
give	gave	see	saw
go	went	take	took

There is a verb in front of each sentence.
● Change the verb to tell about the past.
Write each sentence. Fill in your new verb.

take   1. Mr. Smith __took__ us onto the old train.

go   2. We ____ to the engine.

do   3. The firemen ____ hard work there.

see   4. Then we ____ the coal car.

run   5. Old-time trains ____ on coal.

give   6. Coal ____ the engine its power.

is   7. The trip ____ fun.

learn   8. We ____ many things.

Writing About Machines

A Think of a job you hate to do.

Make up a machine that will do the job.

Use a sheet of drawing paper.

Draw your new machine.

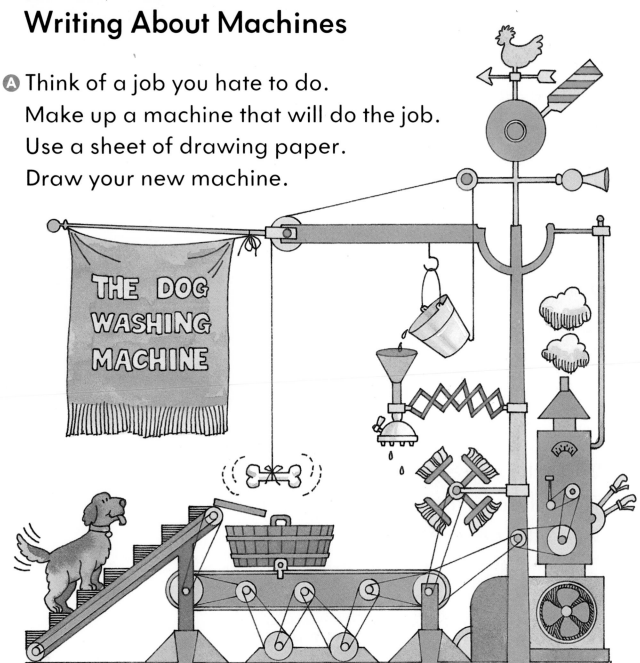

THE DOG
WASHING
MACHINE

Use a sheet of writing paper.

B Write three or more sentences about your machine.

Tell what it is and has and does.

115

Checking Your Skills

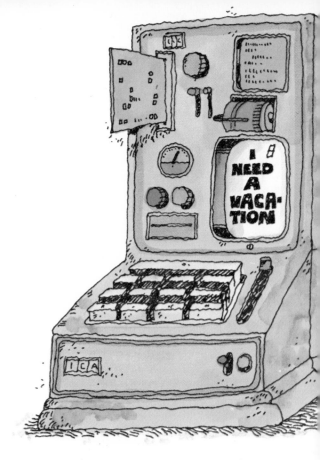

A Write every verb in the following sentences.

A computer is a useful machine. It works for people. People give it directions. The computer follows its directions.

B Write the correct verb for each sentence below. Then change the verb to tell about the past. Write the new verb.

Now	In the Past
1. I (am, is, are) with my friends.	2. ____
3. We (want, wants) some popcorn.	4. ____
5. Sally (go, goes) into the kitchen.	6. ____
7. She (see, sees) the popcorn maker.	8. ____
9. We (has, have) fun making popcorn.	10. ____

Chapter 8 **Writing Book Reports**

● Listen as your teacher reads the story.

A Talk about books. Tell what kinds you like.
Who can help you find books?

true stories

make-believe stories

animal stories

books that tell how
to do something

picture books

The title is the name of the book.
You write titles in a special way.

B Look at the title below. It is written the right way.

The True Book of Snakes

Use a capital letter to begin the first word, the last
word, and every important word of a title.

Draw a line under every word in a title.

C Write each title below the right way.

1. the golden goose   2. millions of cats

118

Learning About Books

A The **author** is the person who wrote the book.
Find the name of each author.

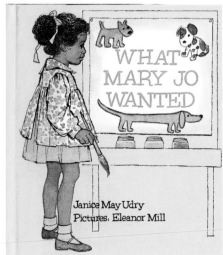

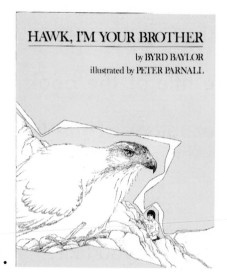

1.

2.

> **Use a capital letter at the beginning**
> **of each part of the author's name.**

B Finish each sentence telling about the books above.
Write the sentences.

1. The title of the first book is ____ .

2. Its author is ____ .

3. The title of the second book is ____ .

4. Its author is ____ .

A Use a writing paper.
Finish these sentences.
Tell about the book in
        the picture.
Use capital letters in
        the right places.

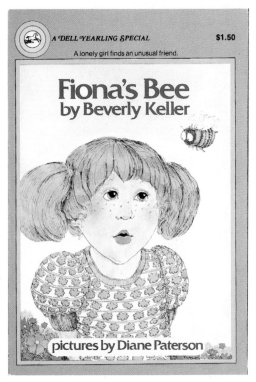

1. The title of the book is ___ .

2. The author of the book is ___ .

B Find a book you like. Finish these sentences.
Write the sentences on your writing paper.

1. The title of my book is _____ .

2. The author is ___ .

Some books have special parts to help you.

C Use this book. Find the parts listed below.
Write the place where you find each, front or back.

1. A list of what is in the book, called
        the table of contents

2. A list of helpful words, called the dictionary

What Is the Book About?

Some books tell stories.

Stories can tell about things
    that really happened.

Stories can tell about things
    that might happen.

Stories can tell about things
    that could not ever happen.

● Write which kind each story is.

really happened   might happen   could not happen

1. <u>Fiona's Bee</u> is about a girl and a bee
   and the girl's new friends.

2. <u>The Bears' Picnic</u> tells about bears who
   talk and go on a picnic.

3. <u>Christopher Columbus</u> tells about what
   Christopher Columbus did long ago.

Some books do not tell stories.

Some books have rhymes.
Some books have riddles or jokes.
Some books tell about real things.

Ⓐ Find a book you like that tells a story.
Write the title on a writing paper.

Ⓑ Copy the right sentence on your paper.

1. This story really happened.

2. This story might have happened.

3. This story could not happen.

122

Thinking About the Story

A story may be about a person.
In most stories the person is not real.
The person is make-believe.
The person acts like a real person.

A story may be about an animal.
In many stories, animals act like people.

Ⓐ Think of <u>Fiona's Bee.</u>
Finish this sentence.
Write the sentence.

<u>Fiona's Bee</u> was about _____.

Ⓑ Think of your book.
Write a sentence about it.
Start with the title. Tell who is in the story.

123

Most stories tell about one important thing
   that happens.
All the parts of the story go together to tell about
   that important thing.

Think about Stone Soup.
The most important thing that happens is this.

   The soldiers trick the people.

Think about Fiona's Bee.
All the parts tell about the most important
   thing that happens.

Ⓐ Find the right ending. Write the sentence.

Fiona's Bee is all about
   1. how Fiona has a dog dish.
   2. how Fiona makes friends.
   3. how Fiona likes bees.

Ⓑ Write one sentence about your book.
Tell the most important thing that happens.

Thinking More About the Story

Most stories did not really happen.
We can tell about them as if they did happen.

We can say this about
    "Hansel and Gretel."

The story happened
    long ago in a forest.

What can we say about <u>Fiona's Bee?</u>

A Write the answers.

1. When ? _____
    A. happened long ago   B. could happen now

2. Where ? _____
    A. in a forest   B. in a town   C. on a farm

What can you say about your story?

B Write when it happened. Write where it happened.

A Here are some things that happen in <u>Fiona's Bee</u>.
Tell which thing is not very important.

A. Fiona finds a bee in her dog dish.

B. She walks down the street with the bee.

C. A boy is riding a bike.

D. Other children talk to Fiona about the bee.

E. Fiona lets the bee crawl onto her shoulder.

F. She makes friends with the other children.

B Read the sentences that are important.
Which thing happened first in the story?
Which happened second? Which happened next?
Read the sentences in the right order.

C Now think about your book.
What happened first? What happened next?
Write about five very important things
    that happened.
Write them in the order they happened.
Save your paper.

Writing a Book Report

When you tell about a book, tell these things.

1. What is the title?
2. Who is the author?
3. Who is in the story?
4. What is the most important thing that happens?
5. Tell some things that happened, in order.
6. Why do you like the book?

● Read Tony's report.
Find where he answered the six questions.

Fiona's Bee is by Beverly Keller. It tells how a girl named Fiona made friends. She finds a bee in her dog dish and saves it. She carries the bee on her shoulder. Children talk to her about the bee. They become her friends. I liked the story because I like bees, too.

A Write your book report.
Be sure to answer all six questions.
Use your list of things that happened
    in the story.

---

1. What is the title?
2. Who is the author?
3. Who is in the story?
4. What is the most important thing
    that happens?
5. Tell some things that happened, in order.
6. Why do you like the book?

B Draw a picture of the story.
Show something you told about in your report.

Giving a Book Report

Tony is giving his book
    report to his class.
He read his report.
He showed his book.
Now he is showing the
    picture he made.

A Get ready to give your report.

    Be sure your report is done.
    Be sure you can read your report.
    Have a copy of the book.
    Choose one or two pictures from the book to show.
    Have your picture of the story to show.

B When you give your report, do these things.

    Speak clearly.
    Speak loudly enough for all to hear you.

C Listen quietly when others give their reports.

Checking Your Skills

A Choose the right ending for each sentence.
Write the sentences.

          A. the name of the book.

1. The author is

          B. a person in the story.

2. The title is

          C. the person who wrote the book.

B Write these titles.
Use capital letters correctly. Use underlining correctly.

1. Becky and the bear

2. the story of Babar

C Write which kind each story is.

really happened   might happen   could not happen

1. <u>George Washington</u> tells about
what George Washington did.

2. <u>The Witch's Vacation</u> tells about
a vacation for a friendly witch.

Chapter 9 Pronouns

● Listen as your teacher reads the story.
Can you find any heroes in the picture?

Here is a sentence about the story.
The nouns are in blue.

Jasper put pictures on the board.

You can use other words in place of the nouns.

He put them on it.

Ⓐ Write the word used in place of each noun.

1. Jasper   2. pictures   3. the board

A word that takes the place of a noun is a pronoun.

Ⓑ Five sentences below use nouns. Five use pronouns.
Find the pronouns. Write the pronouns.

1. Jasper talked to people. He talked to people.

2. People asked questions. They asked questions.

3. He answered the questions. He answered them.

4. Jasper helped his mother. Jasper helped her.

5. Mother thought that Father was a hero.
   She thought that Father was a hero.

Using I and Me

Pat went to the beach.
Dad took Pat there.

I went to the beach.
Dad took me there.

When you talk about yourself, most of the time
you do not use your own name.
Instead you use I or me.

> Use I if your name would be the naming part.
> Use me if your name would come in other places.

● Choose the right pronoun.
Write I or me for each sentence.

1. ＿＿＿ like the beach.

2. Mom and Dad take ＿＿＿ into the water.

3. They are teaching ＿＿＿ to swim.

4. ＿＿＿ cannot swim well yet.

Ⓐ Look at the blue words. Find the pronouns.

Dad and I save shells.

Dad and I found some new ones today.

Mom gave Dad and me some good ones, too.

> Write the word I with a capital letter.
>
> When you talk about yourself and others,
> name yourself last.

Ⓑ Write these sentences about yourself and a friend.
Use the friend's name in one place.
Use I or me in the other place.

1. ___ and ___ have new bikes.
2. ___ and ___ take care of our bikes.
3. Mom let ___ and ___ ride to the park.
4. ___ and ___ rode down Main Street.
5. Friends played with ___ and ___ .

Using We and Us

You can talk about yourself and someone else in two ways.

You can name the other person and use I or me for yourself.

> **Examples**   Jodie and I helped Mom.
> Mom thanked Jodie and me.

You can use we or us.

> **Examples**   We helped Mom.
> Mom thanked us.

> **Use we for the naming part.**
> **Use us for other parts.**

● Use the correct pronoun. Write we or us.

1. Mom asked ___ to clean up.
2. ___ raked leaves on Friday.
3. Can ___ take in the chairs?
4. Mom made lemonade for ___ .
5. There were cookies for ___ , too.

Use we or us in place of the blue words.
● Write the sentences.

1. Terry and I like to help people.

2. Mr. King was happy to see Terry and me.

3. He wanted Terry and me to carry a box.

4. Terry and I picked up the box.

5. Then Terry and I put it in the yard.

6. Mr. King thanked Terry and me.

136

Pronouns as the Naming Part of the Sentence

Use these pronouns as the naming part of a sentence.

One	More than One
I	we
you	you
he	they
she	
it	

● Read the words before each sentence.

Which pronoun can take the place of those words in the sentence?

Write the sentence. Fill in the naming part.

Use the correct pronoun.

Example The weather __It__ was cold.

Kim, Don, and I   1. ___ met a girl.

The girl   2. ___ had lost a mitten.

The mitten   3. ___ was in the snow.

Kim and Don   4. ___ wanted to help.

Kim   5. ___ found the mitten.

Don   6. ___ took it to the girl's home.

Pronouns in Other Parts of the Sentence

These pronouns may not be used
    as the naming part of the sentence.
Use them in other parts of the sentence.

One	More than One
me	us
him	them
her	

These pronouns may be used anywhere
    in a sentence.

One	More than One
you	you
it	

● Change all the blue words to pronouns.
Write the sentences.

1. Pam and Bill helped Mrs. Fox.
2. Mrs. Fox dropped a book.
3. Pam put the book back.
4. The book was not hurt.
5. Mrs. Fox thanked Pam and Bill.
6. She asked Jean and me to help next week.

138

Writing About a Hero

A Think about someone who is a hero to you.
A hero can be famous.
A hero can be someone only you know.
Draw your hero on drawing paper.

Use writing paper.
B Write three or more sentences about your hero.
Use at least three pronouns in your sentences.

Checking Your Skills

Ⓐ Write I or me for each sentence.

1. ___ cross the street safely.

2. The school guard helps ___ .

3. My little brother and ___ walk home together.

4. Mother gives him and ___ a snack.

5. She trusts ___ to watch him on the way.

Ⓑ Write a pronoun to take the place of the blue words.
Use any of these pronouns.

> I, we, you   me, us, you
> he, she, it, they   him, her, it, them

1. This pencil is red.

2. Give it to your father.

3. Two friends were walking.

4. Please help Carla and me.

5. Joan wore a red dress.

6. Al met the new neighbors.

Chapter 10 Writing a Story

● Listen as your teacher reads the story.
  Have you ever had an adventure like that one?
  Would you like to have an adventure like that?

141

Ⓐ Talk about the story.

Can you remember some things that happened?

What were the most exciting parts?

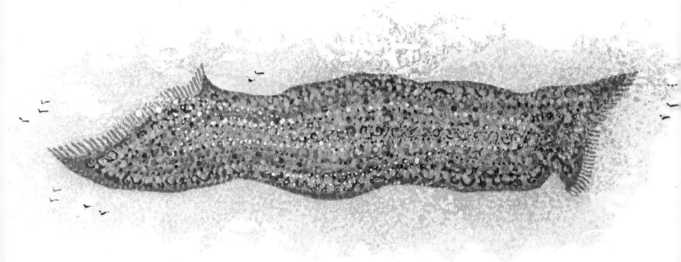

You can write stories, too.

You can tell about real things that happened.

You can tell about make-believe things
    that could happen.

You can tell about things you want to happen.

Begin to think about your story.

Use writing paper.

Ⓑ Write a sentence about something exciting you did.

Ⓒ Write a sentence about a make-believe adventure.

142

Ideas That Go Together

David had a scary walk in the woods.
He wants to write about the walk.
First, he writes what he remembers.
His sentences are out of order.

I heard thunder.

We were at a picnic
last summer.

I walked away by myself.

In winter there is snow
in the woods.

The thunder scared me.

I got lost in the woods.

I found the path back to
the picnic table
before it rained.

● Tell the sentence that
does not belong
with the others.

Think of the story you want to write.

1. Is it real?

   Try to remember the things that happened.

2. Is the story make-believe?

   Think of things that you want to happen in the story.

Ⓐ Write the things you thought of.
Write at least four sentences.
Your sentences may be out of order.

Ⓑ Make sure all your sentences are about your story.
Cross out any sentence that does not belong.
Save your paper.

144

Telling Things in Order

These pictures tell a story. The story is all mixed up.
Put the pictures in order.

A Write A, B, C, and D on your paper.
Then write 1, 2, 3, and 4 in the right places.

  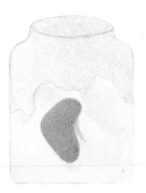 

A. ___   B. ___   C. ___   D. ___

These sentences tell a story.

B Put the sentences in order.
Write A, B, C, D, and E.
Then write 1, 2, 3, 4, and 5 in the right places.

A. __1__   Yesterday it snowed.
B. ___   Then I went outside.
C. ___   I put warm clothes on.
D. ___   I made a snowman.
E. __5__   I gave my snowman a shovel.

David is putting his sentences in order.

He is using the list he wrote before.

Ⓐ Put the rest of his sentences in order.

Write the letters A to F on your paper.

Write the numbers 1 to 6 in the right places.

A. ___ I heard thunder.

B. _1_ We were at a picnic last summer.

C. _2_ I walked away by myself.

D. ___ The thunder scared me.

E. _3_ I got lost in the woods.

F. ___ I found the path back to the picnic
table before it rained.

Ⓑ Use the sentences you wrote for your story.

Put your sentences in order.

Write numbers in front of your sentences.

Starting Your Story

Here is Betsy's plan for a make-believe story.

__1__ I got into my space ship.

__2__ The rockets started up.

__3__ Then the ship took off.

__4__ Soon I was high above Earth.

__5__ I went around Earth six times.

Now she needs a title for her story.
The title will tell what the story is about.

Ⓐ Help Betsy choose a title.
Talk about the titles below.
Write the one that you think is best.

　　1.　A Trip

　　2.　A Space Adventure

　　3.　What I Did Yesterday

Ⓑ Think of a title for your story.
Write it on your plan.

147

A good beginning sentence does these things.

It tells a little about the story.
It gets a reader interested in the story.

Ⓐ Help Betsy choose a good beginning sentence.
Talk about the sentences below.
Write the one that you think is best.

1. This is a make-believe story.

2. I watch stars in the sky at night.

3. My first trip to space was exciting.

Ⓑ Look at your plan.
Does your first sentence do its job?
If you like, write a new beginning sentence.
Add it to your plan.

Now Betsy can write her story.
She will write the sentences from her plan, in order.
She will not copy the numbers that tell the order.

Writing Your Story

A You are ready to write your story.

Use your plan.
If you have a better story idea, make a new plan for it.
Your title is on the plan.
The plan tells what comes first.
It tells what comes second, and third, and so on.
You may add sentences, too.
Be sure that they belong in the story.

B Follow these rules.

> **Begin every sentence with a capital letter.**
> **Begin every proper noun with a capital letter.**
>
> **End every statement or command with a period.**
> **End every question with a question mark.**
> **End every exclamation with an exclamation mark.**

C If you like, draw a picture for
   your story.

149

Ending Your Story

Every story needs an ending sentence.
A good ending sentence tells one of these things.

1. It tells how the story turned out.
2. It tells why the story was important.
3. It tells what the writer thinks.
4. It tells how the writer feels.

Ⓐ Help Betsy choose a good ending sentence.
Talk about the sentences below.
Write the one that you think is best.

1. At last I landed in my backyard.

2. That's the end of the story.

3. The spaceship was blue.

Ⓑ Write a good ending sentence for your story.
Add it to your story.

150

Making Your Story Better

David read his story to himself.
He found some things that could be better.
David marked his changes. Then he made a clean copy.

A Scary Picnic
We were at a picknic last summer.
I walkeded away by myself. I got
lost in the woods. The thunder
I heard thunder.
scared me. I found the path back
to the picnic table before it rained.
Every body was happy to see me.

● Go over your story. Look for these things.
Then mark changes and make a clean copy.

1. Do all the sentences belong?
2. Are the sentences in the right order?
3. Are the beginning and ending sentences good?
4. Did I follow the writing rules for sentences and proper nouns?
5. Did I spell all the words the right way?

151

Checking Your Skills

A Here are the steps for writing a story.
The steps are out of order.
One sentence does not belong.

Choose the steps that belong together.
Write the numbers 1 to 5 on your paper.
Then write the sentences in the right order.

> A. You write sentences about what happened.
>
> B. You watch TV.
>
> C. First you find your idea.
>
> D. You put your sentences in order.
>
> E. You mark changes and make a clean copy.
>
> F . Then you write good beginning and
>   ending sentences.

B Here are three beginning sentences.
Write the best one.

> Star was a magic dog.
> This is a story about a magic dog.
> Some people like dogs.

Chapter 11 Words That Describe

● Listen as your teacher reads the story. Talk about it.

What special things have you found?

What other things are special to you?

153

These children are telling about special things.

Use drawing paper.

Ⓐ Draw their special things as well as you can.

> I have a toy.
> I got it for my
> birthday. I like it.

> My shell is big
> and round. It is
> bumpy and white
> outside. It is pink
> and shiny inside.

Ⓑ Show your pictures. Talk about them.

Did everyone draw the same kind of toy?

Did everyone draw the same kind of shell?

Which words told you what to put into the pictures?

Words like big, round, and bumpy are describing words.

Words That Tell How Many

Some words tell more about nouns.
They tell how many.

Examples   **some** nouns   **two** words

A Write the words from the picture
    that tell how many.

many balls

1. ____

2. ____

3. ____

one ball

three balls

B Draw five squares. Color some of the squares red.
Write these sentences.
Fill in describing words words that tell how many.

1. I colored ____ squares red.
2. I did not color ____ squares.

Words That Tell What Color

Some words tell what color a thing is.

A Write these sentences about the picture below.
Fill in the color words.

1. ___ and ___ flowers grow in my garden.
2. I saw a ___ bird near my flowers.
3. A ___ squirrel sat on the ___ grass.

B Write only the color words in these sentences.

1. Our flag is red, white, and blue.

2. Cars stop for red lights, and go past green lights.

Words That Tell About the Look of a Thing

Color words tell how a thing looks.
Other words do, too.

● Write all the words in the story below
   that tell how a thing looks.

The people wore shiny suits. They climbed the high steps to the open door. The huge crowd cheered. A large bright flame came from the rocket. The big spaceship took off.

Words That Tell the Feel of a Thing

Each group of words below tells how things feel.

Ⓐ In each group, write four words that go together.

A	B	C
1. hot	1. smooth	1. hard
2. warm	2. sandy	2. three
3. cool	3. orange	3. soft
4. cold	4. rough	4. strong
5. tall	5. furry	5. weak

Ⓑ Talk about the words.
How do the words in each group go together?

Ⓒ Write two words about each thing below.
Tell how these things feel.
Use words from the groups above.
More than two words may be right.

1. marble

2. pudding

3. mouse

4. rock

Words That Tell About Sound or Smell

These words tell
how a thing sounds.

These words tell
how a thing smells.

loud	sweet
quiet	fresh
noisy	smoky

Each picture below shows something that has a
sound or a smell.

A Write a word that describes the smell.

1.

2.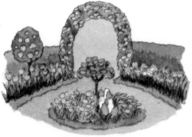

3.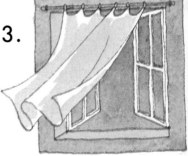

B Write a word that describes the sound.

4.

5.

6.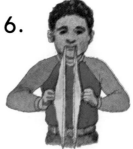

159

Words That Tell About Taste

1.

2.

3.

4.

5.

● Write a sentence about each food.
Tell how it tastes.

juicy   salty   sour   spicy   sweet

1. _____

2. _____

3. _____

4. _____

5. _____

Words That Compare Two Things

Some describing words compare two things.

cold

colder

> **Add er to a describing word that compares two people or two things.**

● Write a describing word that compares the two things.

1. tall   1. ___

3. loud   3. ___

2. small   2. ___

4. long   4. ___

161

Words That Compare Three or More Things

Some describing words compare three or more things.

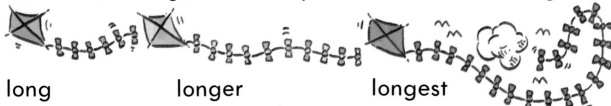

long   longer   longest

> **Add est to a describing word that compares three or more things.**

● Write the describing word that compares all three.

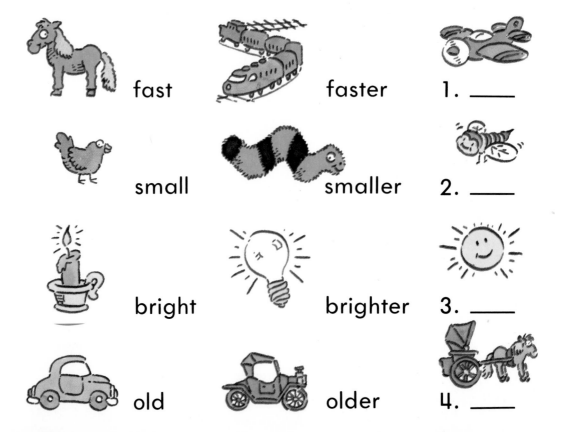

fast   faster   1. ____

small   smaller   2. ____

bright   brighter   3. ____

old   older   4. ____

Words That Tell About Actions

Some words describe **how** a thing acts.

slowly   softly   carefully

Some words describe **when** a thing acts.

today   now   often

Some words describe **where** a thing acts.

here   up   nearby

● Read each word in the orange box.
Write each word in the right group.

easily	**there**	**away**
yesterday	**loudly**	**always**
then	**down**	**quickly**

How a thing acts	When a thing acts	Where a thing acts
1. _____	1. _____	1. _____
2. _____	2. _____	2. _____
3. _____	3. _____	3. _____

163

This story uses words that tell about actions.
● Find the words that tell how and when and where.
Write those words.

A Little Mouse

Yesterday a little mouse and his mother
went outside. He played happily. Then the
mouse heard a noise. Maybe a cat was
nearby! The mouse ran quickly to his mother.

His mother spoke gently. "Don't worry,"
she said. "We will go inside now. A cat can't
catch us there."

Writing About a Special Thing

Use drawing paper.

Ⓐ Draw a thing that is special to you.

It may be a pet, a toy, or anything else
that is special to you.

Use writing paper.

Ⓑ Write two or three sentences about your special thing.

Use one or more describing words in each sentence.

Checking Your Skills

Copy the blue words and the numbers.
● Then write each word below in the right group.

red	five	spicy	sour
shiny	badly	yellow	loud
two	salty	new	sadly
quickly	bright	noisy	some
quiet	purple		

How many

1. ____
2. ____
3. ____

What color

4. ____
5. ____
6. ____

The look of a thing

7. ____
8. ____
9. ____

The sound of a thing

10. ____
11. ____
12. ____

The taste of a thing

13. ____
14. ____
15. ____

How a thing acts

16. ____
17. ____
18. ____

Chapter 12 **Writing a Description**

● Listen as your teacher reads the story.

What does an ant look like? What does an ant feel like?

167

Ⓐ Talk about the story.

Could you imagine you are an ant?

Did the story help you imagine that?

How did the story let you know what an ant
     is like? What things did it tell you?

The story was a description of an ant.

It described many things about an ant.

    It told about its size.

    It told about its shape.

    It told about its face.

The description helped you see the ant clearly.

Ⓑ Think of something you would like to describe.

Write the name of that thing.

This chapter will help you.

You will find out how to describe a thing clearly.

Planning How To Describe Something

How would you describe
   a giant?
You would probably start
   with his feet.
Then you would move up
   to his head.

A Choose the right ending.
Write the sentence.

This plan would be   from bottom to top.
                        from front to back.
                        from left to right.

A bottom-to-top plan is good for describing a giant.
It is not good for describing a fried egg.

B Think about the things listed below.
Is a bottom-to-top plan good for each of them?
Write **Yes** or **No**.

1. a tree
2. a football
3. a rocket

4. a watch face
5. a very tall building
6. a grandfather clock

How would you describe a dragon?
You would probably start with the head.
Then you would move back to the tail.

A Choose the right ending.
Write the sentence.

This plan would be   from bottom to top.
                       from front to back.
                       outside to inside.

B Think about the things listed below.
Which plan would be good for describing each thing?
Choose from these plans. Write **A**, **B**, or **C**.

    Plan **A**—bottom to top
    Plan **B**—front to back
    Plan **C**—outside to inside

1. a train   3. a flagpole   5. a caterpillar

2. an apple   4. a mountain   6. a bird's nest

170

Reading a Description

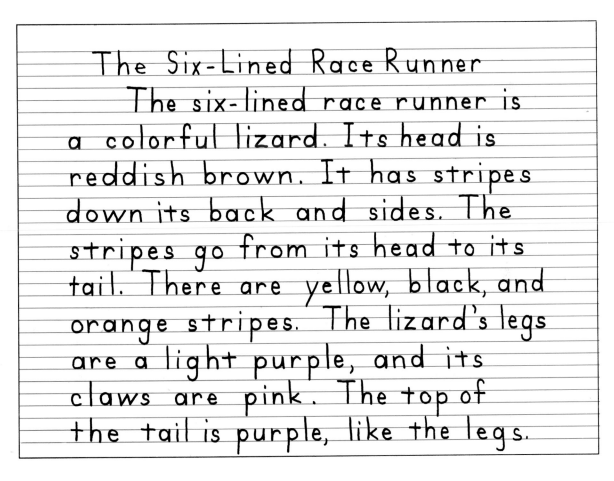

● Read this description carefully.
Then write the answer to each question below.

> **The Six-Lined Race Runner**
> The six-lined race runner is a colorful lizard. Its head is reddish brown. It has stripes down its back and sides. The stripes go from its head to its tail. There are yellow, black, and orange stripes. The lizard's legs are a light purple, and its claws are pink. The top of the tail is purple, like the legs.

1. What does the description tell about?
2. Which part is reddish brown?
3. Which parts have stripes?
4. What does the description say about the tail?
5. What plan does the description use?

Writing a Description

● Follow these steps for writing
　a description.

1. Choose the thing you will write about.

2. Choose a plan for describing it.

3. Write sentences about the thing.
　Use words that describe.
　Make sure that all the sentences belong.
　Make sure that they are in the right
　　order for your plan.

4. Write a title.

5. If you like, draw a picture for
　your story.

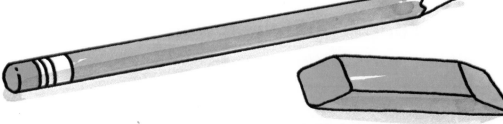

Making Your Work Better

Now you have written a description.

A Go over your paper. Ask yourself these questions.

Does my description make sense?

1. Do all the sentences belong?

2. Are the sentences in the right order?

3. Does the beginning sentence tell what I am writing about?

4. Is the ending sentence good?

5. Did I use words that describe?

6. Does each sentence tell an idea?

Have I written my description clearly?

1. Does each sentence begin with a capital letter?

2. Does each sentence end with a period or a question mark?

3. Does each proper noun begin with a capital letter?

4. Is each word spelled the right way?

B Correct your mistakes. Make a clean copy.

Checking Your Skills

This description has several mistakes.
- Copy the description, just as it is.
Then follow the directions below.

A banana split haz three
parts. at the bottom is a
sliced banana Too scoops of ice
cream sit on top of it. chocolate
syrup runs over the ice cream.
Every part tastes good.

1. Which plan was used? Write the answer.
   bottom to top   left to right   inside to outside

2. Two words that should have capital letters do not.
   Find those words. Draw a line under each.

3. There should be another period. Put it in.

4. Two words have the wrong spelling. Circle them.
   Then write them correctly below the description.

174

Handbook

When you write, you must use capital letters in certain places. Do you know where to use them?

You use a period at the end of some sentences. You use a question mark or exclamation point at the end of other sentences. Do you know which one to use?

There are other marks to use in writing, too. Do you know when to use them?

This Handbook will help you answer the questions. Here is what the Handbook tells about.

page 176—Using Capital Letters for Special Words
page 177—Using Capital Letters for First Words
page 178—Using the Period
page 179—Using the Question Mark and
　　　　　　　Exclamation Point
page 180—Using the Comma
page 181—Using the Apostrophe
page 182—Writing Titles of Books

If you have questions about these things in your writing, find the answers in this Handbook.

Using Capital Letters for Special Words

Rule 1. Write the word **I** with a capital letter.
Soon I will be nine years old.

Rule 2. Begin every word in a proper noun
with a capital letter.

A. The name of a person or pet is a proper
noun.

John Bates   Mrs. Key   Flicka

B. The name of a place is a proper noun.
Jackson School   Green Road
Carson City   America

C. The name of a day or a month is a proper
noun.

Saturday   Labor Day   April

● Write these sentences. Use capital letters correctly.

1. May i go with angela?
2. Please give frisky some milk.
3. Yes, mr. ed waters is our neighbor.
4. On tuesday nina visited kent school.
5. Cousin joan lives in ames, iowa.
6. Yesterday i walked down pine tree road.

Using Capital Letters for First Words

Rule 1. Begin every sentence with a capital letter.

This cat is friendly.

Who answered the phone?

Ⓐ Write these sentences. Use capital letters correctly.

1. the glue is not dry yet.
2. catch that dog!
3. how soon will we go home?
4. a week has seven days.
5. two of us fell on the ice.
6. please save a seat for me.

Rule 2. Begin the first word in the greeting or the closing of a letter with a capital letter.

Greeting Dear Ellen,

Closing Your friend,

Ⓑ Write these letter parts. Use capital letters correctly.

1. dear Tom,
2. your niece,
3. dear Uncle Jack,
4. dear Paula,
5. your loving son,
6. yours truly,

Using the Period

Rule 1.   Use a period at the end of a statement.

Today is Wednesday.

Rule 2.   Use a period at the end of a command.

Bring your favorite game.

A Write these sentences. Use periods correctly.

1. Becky might win this race
2. Don't forget your lunch
3. Mike came to school early
4. This puzzle is not hard
5. Meet me at the park
6. Turn right at Hill Street

Rule 3.   Use a period at the end of these titles.

Mr.   Ms.   Mrs.

B Write these names. Use periods correctly.

1. Ms Lisa Jones   3. Mr Franklin   5. Mr Sam Yee
2. Mrs Ortiz   4. Miss Paul   6. Ms Harper

Using the Question Mark and Exclamation Point

Rule 1.   Use a question mark at the end
of a question.
Who is at the door?

Rule 2.   Use an exclamation point at the end of a
sentence that shows strong feeling.
How hot it is today!

● Write each sentence. It may be a statement, a
command, a question, or an exclamation. Use the
correct mark at the end of the sentence.

1. What are we having for dinner
2. Answer this riddle
3. What a strong smell that onion has
4. The library is open now
5. Are these your gloves
6. Visit us next week
7. What good cookies you bake
8. Please help me with this job
9. I like the red flowers best
10. Do you want to play

Using the Comma

Rule 1. Use a comma in an address between the name of a city and the name of a state or country.

San Diego, California   London, England

Rule 2. Use a comma in a date between the day and the year.

June 14, 1983   April 1, 1984

Ⓐ Write these sentences. Use commas correctly.

1. Our trip began on July 26 1982.

2. Laura lives in Cleveland Ohio.

3. This letter came from Rome Italy.

4. Ben was born February 2 1975.

5. My neighbors moved to Austin Texas.

6. Did you live here on December 19 1981?

Rule 3. Use a comma after the greeting of a letter. (The greeting is the part that says who gets the letter.)

Dear Carlos,   My dear friend,

Rule 4. Use a comma after the closing of a letter. (The closing is the way you say goodbye before you write your name.)

Your daughter,   Sincerely,

B Write these parts of a letter. Use commas correctly.

1. Your best friend
2. Dear Aunt Kathy
3. March 4 1985

4. Dear Grandpa
5. Kansas City Kansas
6. Your neighbor

Using the Apostrophe

Rule. Use an apostrophe in a contraction to show where letters have been left out.

is not = isn't   I am = I'm
did not = didn't   she will = she'll
have not = haven't   it is = it's
would not = wouldn't   he would = he'd

● Form contractions of these words. Write the contractions. Use apostrophes in the right places.

1. have not
2. she will

3. he would
4. is not

5. it is
6. did not

Writing Titles of Books

Rule 1.   Use capital letters to begin the first word, the last word, and every important word of a title.

<u>A Rocket in My Pocket</u>
<u>The Tale of Benjamin Bunny</u>

Rule 2.   Underline the title of a book.

<u>The Little Fire Engine</u>
<u>The Cat in the Hat</u>

● Write these titles of books. Use capital letters and underlining correctly.

1. my father's dragon
2. the tale of two bad mice
3. mommies at work
4. little bear's visit
5. the wind in the willows
6. where the wild things are
7. madeline and the bad hat
8. a house in the country

Dictionary

A a

airplane

airport   a place that airplanes fly to and from

alligator

animal   any living being that moves by itself, such as an ant, a fish, a bird, or a dog

ant

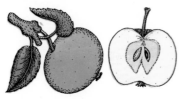

apartment house   a building where many families live

apple
a fruit

applesauce   a sauce made by cooking apples

arm   a part of the body

ate   (past of **eat**)
Last night we **ate** chicken.

author   a person who writes a book, poem, or story

B b

baker   a person who bakes

ball

balloon

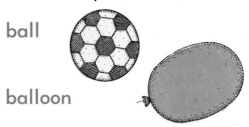

banana
a fruit

bark (verb)   to make a noise like a dog

bark (noun)   the outside covering of a tree

bee

bicycle or **bike**

black
a color

blue
a color

boat

boy

bread

C c

cake

carpet   a rug

carrot

cat

caterpillar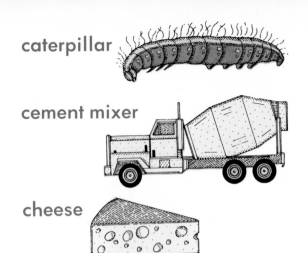

cement mixer

cheese

child   a person younger
than 18

children   more than one
child

circle

city   a very big town

clown

come (**came** in the past)
    Many children **come** to school.
    Mom **came** with me yesterday.

comma   ,

command a sentence that tells or asks someone to do something

cookbook a book that tells how to cook foods

corn a vegetable

D d

daffodil

describe to tell what someone or something is like

do (**did** in the past)
I **do** many jobs at home.
I **did** my work yesterday.

dog

drill

duck

E e

eat (**ate** in the past)
We **eat** three meals each day.

egg

eight the word for 8

elephant

exit the way out

F f

face a part of the body

farm a place where many plants or animals are grown for food

fire

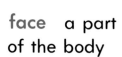

firefighter someone who puts out fires

foot   a part
of the body

or a unit of measuring how
long a thing is. A foot is
twelve inches long.

feet   more than one foot

for   Is this **for** me?

forest   a place filled with
many trees

four   the word for 4

frog

fruit   certain foods from
plants, for example, oranges,
apples, and bananas

G g

garden   a place where flowers
or vegetables are grown

gift   a present

girl

give (**gave** in the past)
    The sun **gives** us light.
    I **gave** Ann some of my lunch.

go (**went** in the past)
    I **go** to school every day.
    I **went** to the zoo last week.

grapes
a fruit

grass

green
a color

guard   a person who keeps
things or people safe

gym   an indoor place for sports

H h

hand   a part of the body

have   (**had** in the past)
    I **have** a new bike.
    We **had** a surprise yesterday.

head   a part
of the body

hear to receive sounds by your ears

heart a shape

or a part of the body

helicopter

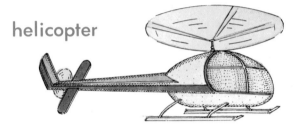

here in this place

house

I i

I a word for naming yourself

ice

ice cream

inch a unit of measuring how long a thing is

1"

iron

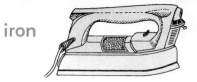

J j

jack-o'-lantern

jeep

jet

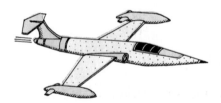

job the work that someone does

K k

kangaroo

key

king

kitchen   a room for cooking

kite

know (**knew** in the past)
   I **know** that person.
   No one **knew** the answer.

L l

lake

leaf

   leaves   more than one leaf

leg
a part
of the body

lemon
a fruit

lettuce
a vegetable

library   a place where many
books are kept

lime
a fruit

line ———————————

lion

lunch   a meal eaten in the
middle of the day

lunchbox   a box for carrying
lunch

M m

man

   men   more than one man

meat

meatball   a ball made from ground meat

meet   to get to know
   We **meet** people at school.
or to join
   I will **meet** you in the park.

milk

monkey

moon
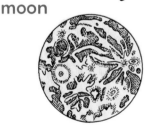

mountain

mouse

mice   more than one mouse

N n

needle
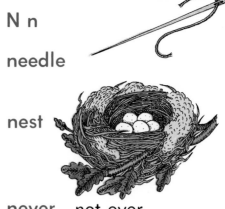

nest

never   not ever

new   not old

newspaper   a paper that tells the news

night   not day

nuts

O o

oatmeal   a cereal made from oats

ocean   sea

one   the word for 1

orange
a fruit
or the color
of that fruit

owl

P p

pancakes

parent   a mother or father

park

peach
a fruit

pear
a fruit

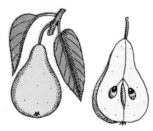

period   •

picnic   a meal eaten outside

pig

pink
a color

plain   not fancy

plane   an airplane

plum
a fruit
or the color of that fruit

police

popcorn

pumpkin
a vegetable

puppet

puppy   a young dog

Q q

queen

question   an asking sentence

question mark   **?**

R r

rabbit

radish
a vegetable

rain

rectangle

red
a color

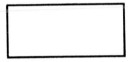

river

rocket

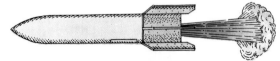

roll (noun)

roll (verb)   to move the way
a ball does

row (noun)   a number of people
or things in a line

row (verb)   to move a boat
with oars

run (**ran** in the past)
     Horses **run** fast.
     I **ran** all the way home.

S s

sailboat

salad

sandwich

school   a place for teaching
and learning

scissors

see (**saw** in the past)
     I **see** a train coming.
     We **saw** a rainbow last week.

191

shoes

skates

snowman

snowmen   more than one snowman

soldier   a person in an army

soup

sour   not sweet

spaceship

square

squirrel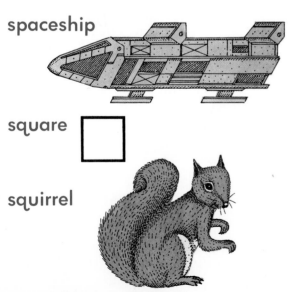

star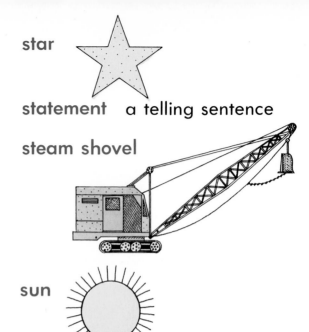

statement   a telling sentence

steam shovel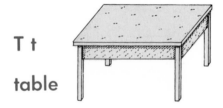

sun

sweet   tasting like sugar

T t

table

tablecloth   a covering for a table

take (**took** in the past)
Birds **take** twigs for nests.
I **took** Mike a gift yesterday.

teach (**taught** in the past)
to show or help to learn how
to do something

teacher   a person who teaches someone

192

tire

title   the name of a book, story, or poem

to   I ride my bike **to** school.

toaster

too   You put **too** much jam on my toast.

town   a place where many people live

train (noun)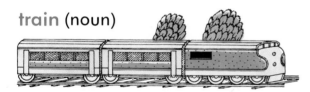

train (verb)   to teach a person or pet

triangle

two   the word for 2

U u

umbrella

V v

valentine   a card sent to a friend on Valentine's Day, or a heart-shaped decoration

vegetables   certain foods from plants, for example, lettuce, potatoes, and beans

violin

W w

wall

watch (noun)

watch (verb)   to look at carefully

wheel

white
a color

win (**won** in the past)
The best player **wins** the prize.

193

wind (noun, rhymes with *pinned*) blowing air

wind (verb, rhymes with *find*) to move in a rolling or twisting way

woman

women   more than one woman

won   past of **win**
We **won** the last game.

wood   material made by a tree

woods   a forest

would   I **would** like to go with you.

X x

xylophone

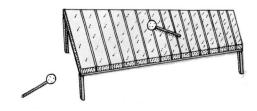

Y y

yard
a place or a unit of measuring how long a thing is. A yard is three feet long.

yarn

yellow
a color

young   not old

Z z

zebra

zigzag

zipper

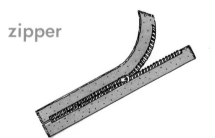

zoo   a place where live animals are kept

Stories for Good Listening

The following stories and poems are to be read by the teacher to introduce the chapters of *Building English Skills, Plum Level*. These selections are provided for the convenience of the teacher.

Chapter 1 (page 1):

Busy Day, Busy People   by Tibor Gergely

It's morning in the city! People are hurrying to work and to school. Some stop to watch the construction workers who are already busy digging and hauling dirt, mixing and pouring cement, lifting and lowering pipes. A new building is just beginning!

City shops and stores are open for another busy day! People come to the drugstore to buy medicine. The pharmacists measure out the right amount.

The food people buy in the city comes from farms far away. This morning a farmer is up in his helicopter. He will check all his fields before he comes down. Many people work on one farm. Fields have to be plowed and planted. Crops have to be picked and stored in trucks to be taken away. Every day there is more work to be done!

In the city the department store is having a busy day, too. Crowds of people hurry in to buy things. Everybody wants help right away! Salespeople see that they find what they want.

At the hospital people are busy helping people get well.

Many different people work in a hospital. Doctors, nurses, technicians, surgeons, ambulance drivers, nurses' aides—everybody helps in an important way!

Chapter 2 (page 15):

Stone Soup, An Old Tale   by Marcia Brown

[Three hungry soldiers, walking home from a war, came to a town. They hoped the people in the town would give them food. But the people hid all their food and told the soldiers they had nothing for themselves.]

So the first soldier said, "We'll have to make stone soup."

The peasants stared.

"First we'll need a large iron pot," the soldiers said, "and water to fill it and a fire to heat it."

It took many buckets of water to fill the pot. A fire was built and the pot was set to boil.

"And now, please, three round, smooth stones."

"Stones like these generally make good soup. But oh, if there were carrots, it would be much better."

"Why, I think I have a carrot or two," said one woman, and off she ran. She came back with her apron full of carrots.

"If we only had a bit of beef and a few potatoes, this soup would be good enough for the king."

The peasants thought that over. They remembered the potatoes and the beef they had hidden. They ran to fetch them.

Never had the peasants tasted such soup. And fancy, made from stones!

Chapter 3 (page 31):

My Sister and I   by Helen E. Buckley

My sister and I
My sister and I
Are swinging and swinging
Up to the sky.

When you have a sister
You can have fun
Playing games for two
Instead of for one:
Hopscotch and catch
And Skip-to-my-Lou
And when it's time to go in
Your sister goes too.

And sometimes your sister and you
Have a fight
Over taking turns
And which one is right;

And before you know it
There is your mother
Asking you
To be nice to each other.

Tra-la-la-la
Tra-la-la-lay
Such a funny song
We are singing today!

195

Chapter 4 (page 55):

A Day at the Beach   by Mircea Vasiliu

It's fun to go the beach on a summer morning. We carry a picnic basket and a cooler. We take folding chairs and towels to lie on, and an umbrella to shade us from too much sun. We'll spend the whole day at the beach.

The first thing we do is dash into the ocean. We swim and splash and pretend to be whales spouting water.

The lifeguard watches for big waves, and for swimmers who have gone too far out to sea.

When we are tired of swimming, we play in the sand.

Waves bring all sorts of things to the beach—sea glass and bottles, shells and smooth stones, and beautiful pieces of driftwood.

Twice a day the tide flows in and the water covers most of the sand. When the tide goes out, the beach is wide again.

We love to walk along the beach and pick up polished stones and pieces of driftwood. The flat stones are best for skipping on the water. We also look for pretty shells to take home.

The tide has gone out, leaving all kinds of plants and animals along the shore. These need sea water to stay alive, but they can spend some time on the beach.

A starfish is a sea animal that looks like a star, but isn't really a fish. If it lies on the sand too long it dies, and its thin, spiny skin dries out. Then we can take the dried starfish home.

Chapter 5 (page 67):

City ABC's   by Michael Deasy

A is for alley.
The alley
Cuts the block in two.
Come with me.
We'll shortcut through.

B is for bridge.
In giant steps
Bridges stretch
Over hushed rivers.

C is for crane.
Cranes
Move and lift,
Hoist and shift,
Heavy weights
For building buildings.

D is for dump.
Shovels heap clumps
From dumps into trucks.
Trucks cart junk away.

E is for escalator
Glide down through
    the store,
Step to the floor,
Turn the corner.

Chapter 6 (page 85):

Anatole and the Cat   by Eve Titus

In all France there was no mouse more honored or respected than Anatole.

He was very proud of his job as Cheese Taster at the factory of M'sieu Duval.

Nobody knew that he was not a man but a mouse, not even M'sieu Duval, for he did his work after the others went home.

One night he entered the Cheese-Tasting Room with Gaston, his good friend and helper.

Anatole tasted some Brie, and made a face. "Too salty! Give me a NOT SO GOOD sign, and I'll write it down."

Just then they heard soft footsteps on the floor above. "IT IS A CAT!" cried Anatole. "Still, we must do our job. As long as he stays upstairs—we work."

They did their best, but they were much too frightened! Then they ran for the window—the cat was on the stairs! The next night, Anatole went to M'sieu Duval's office and typed a memo.

from   ANATOLE
  to   HENRI DUVAL
about   CATS

There are some who dislike dogs, or goldfish, or parakeets. Myself, I do not care for cats.

Last night one of these creatures was in your factory. I was so disturbed that my work was not as good as usual.

If a cat again appears, I may be forced to give up my job, much as I enjoy working for you.

This he left in the typewriter.

The next night there was a second memo from M'sieu Duval in reply to the memo from Anatole.

from   HENRI DUVAL
  to   ANATOLE
about   MY CAT

Now I know where our family pet was the other night.

I have scolded him, and he has strict orders not to remain in the factory after dark. I hope that henceforth you will be able to work in peace.

MERCI BEAUCOUP!

196

Chapter 7 (page 97):

Mike Mulligan and His Steam Shovel
by Virginia Lee Burton

Mike Mulligan had a steam shovel, a beautiful red steam shovel. Her name was Mary Anne. Mike Mulligan was very proud of Mary Anne.

Mike Mulligan and Mary Anne had been digging together for years and years.

It was Mike Mulligan and Mary Anne and some others who dug the great canals for the big boats to sail through.

It was Mike Mulligan and Mary Anne and some others who cut through the high mountains so that trains could go through.

It was Mike Mulligan and Mary Anne and some others who lowered the hills and straightened the curves to make the long highways for the automobiles.

It was Mike Mulligan and Mary Anne and some others who smoothed out the ground and filled in the holes to make the landing fields for the airplanes.

And it was Mike Mulligan and Mary Anne and some others who dug the deep holes for the cellars of the tall sky-scrapers in the big cities. When people used to stop and watch them, Mike Mulligan and Mary Anne used to dig a little faster and a little better. The more people stopped, the faster and the better they dug.

Chapter 8 (page 117):

Fiona's Bee   by Beverly Keller

Fiona Foster went outside to fill her dog dish. Fiona did not have a dog. Every day she put the dog dish on her front porch and filled it with water.

She was hoping that some dog might drop by for a drink, and stay for a few minutes, and be her friend. Fiona was hoping that the dog's owner would come for the dog, and stay for an hour or two, and be her friend. That way Fiona would get two friends out of filling one dog dish. So far, Fiona had no friends.

When Fiona went out to fill her dog dish, there was a bee in the dish! He was swimming around and around in the water at the bottom of the dish. Then he gave up. He just stopped trying and went limp.

Very carefully, Fiona moved a twig under the bee. Then she lifted the twig, with the limp bee on it, out of the dish. She planned to put the bee in a sunny place, and then run. But while she looked for a sunny place, the bee dragged himself up the twig onto her finger! Fiona did not move. The bee held her finger for a minute. He was very small, and very wet, and very, very tired.

After a time he seemed to feel better. He crawled up her arm until he got to her shoulder. Then he settled down, as if the climb had tired him all over again.

[Fiona decided to walk very carefully to the park, where the bee was sure to fly off to the flowers.] In fifteen minutes she walked three blocks. A girl close to Fiona's size was crossing the street. The girl looked at Fiona. Then she said, "Yike! don't move. There'a bee on your shoulder."

"I know," Fiona said.

The girl's eyes got round as a dog dish.

"You *know*?"

"I saved him from drowning."

"Wow." The girl peered at the bee.

A boy on a bicycle stopped at the corner. The girl said to him, "Look. This bee rides on this girl's shoulder because she saved him from drowning."

"Wow." The boy stared at the bee, then at Fiona. "I never knew anybody who had a *bee*," he said.

[The boy and girl told Fiona their names and joined her on her walk to the park. More of their friends came along, too. Finally they got to the park. The bee flew away, but Fiona and her new friends stayed together to play.]

Chapter 9 (page 131):

Jasper and the Hero Business   by Betty Horvath

Jasper lived in the house on the corner. All day long people passed by. Sometimes they stopped and talked to him. There was one question that EVERYBODY asked him. "What are you going to be when you grow up?"

"I'm going to be a hero," Jasper said.

And then they laughed.

"Wait and see," thought Jasper. "Someday I am going to be a big hero. I will have my picture in the paper."

That night the newspaper had a picture of a fireman. He was carrying a baby down a ladder. Jasper cut the picture out of the paper.

That's the way his hero board began.

Every time Jasper read about someone being brave he pinned the story to the board on his bedroom wall.

"Someday," said Jasper, "my picture will be up there, too." He was saving a place for it.

"Do you know any heroes?" he asked his mother.

"Look out the window," said his mother. "There is a hero coming up the walk this very minute."

"That's just father," he said. "I never knew he was a hero."

"There are all kinds of heroes," said his mother. "Your father worked hard today to earn money to pay the rent and the grocery bill. Maybe he would rather have gone fishing. It is a lucky family who has a hero like your father."

"Then I will put his picture on my hero board," said Jasper.

So Jasper found a picture of his father. Then he pinned his mother's picture up beside it.

[The rest of the story tells how, eventually, Jasper does a good deed and his family agrees that he too has become a hero.]

Chapter 10 (page 141):

Maila and the Flying Carpet
by Denise and Alain Trez

Maila was a very spoiled little prince. His father the Rajah gave him all the toys and pets he could want, but the boy was not satisfied with them. More than anything else, he wanted a flying carpet.

But flying carpets were very rare in the kingdom, for the secret of how to make them had been lost.

One day as Maila climbed to the window, he slipped on the stairs. To his surprise the carpet came loose and began to float across the room. It was a flying carpet!

Maila wasted no time. He packed some food and set out to see the world. From so high up, his father's kingdom looked very small.

Just sailing along through the air became a little boring, so Maila swooped down to race with a horse. But the horse was faster than the flying carpet.

[After a while, a flock of] birds landed on the carpet. Down went Maila into the choppy sea. It was a magnificent dive.

Maila hung on tight as the carpet soared into the sky again. But as the carpet dried in the sun, it began to shrink. Now that the carpet was so small, it went much faster.

When night fell, Maila didn't know where he was. He waited for the stars and steered by them toward his father's kingdom.

Chapter 11 (page 153):

Sally's Caterpillar   by Anne Rockwell

Summer was nearly over. But right now there was still time for Sally to play. Her friends, Harry and Dorothy, came to play with her.

Suddenly, they saw a little, slippery snake. Harry said it was his, but the snake slid into a patch of milkweed when he tried to catch it.

Sally was very brave, and she went into the milkweed patch to find the snake. But instead of the snake she found a beautiful big caterpillar, sitting on the milkweed leaf. He had stripes of yellow and black, and he crept along on little black feet. Sally thought he was the most beautiful thing she had ever seen, and she watched him on his leaf while

big orange and black butterflies fluttered about overhead. She called Daddy to come look.

"It's a butterfly's baby," Daddy told her. "One of those big monarch butterflies laid her eggs on a milkweed leaf. When the eggs hatched, out came tiny caterpillars. This one has eaten many tender milkweed leaves, and now he is big and fat. Someday he will turn into a butterfly, just like his parents."

Chapter 12 (page 167):

If You Were an Ant   by Barbara Brenner

Now. Here's an idea:
for a little while,
make believe that you're...an ant.

Begin by looking.
Get up close to an ant.
Study it.
Try to put yourself in the ant's *place*.
Think, "How would it be, to be an ant?"

First of all, think small.
The largest ant anywhere
isn't bigger than your little finger.
And some ants are small enough
to hide inside an apple seed.

So imagine yourself very small.

Now think a color.
Black. Blue. Brown. Red.
Yellowish or *greenish*.
An ant could be any of those colors.
What color ant do you want to be?

Next, get into the body of the ant.
Feel your outside—light and tough.
Hard, like a shell. Not soft, like skin.
Notice your new ant shape—
two parts body, one part head,
six legs instead of two.

And your new ant face—
two huge eyes, a mouth,
a pair of scissor jaws
to bite and tear with.
No ears. No nose. Instead,
you have two hairy feelers on your head.
Wave them around.
Like magic wands, they'll catch the smell
of what's around you.

Index

ABC order, 56-60, 66
Addressing envelopes, 91-92
Adjectives, Adverbs. *See* Describing Words.
Alphabetical order. *See* ABC order.
am, is, are, was, were, 105, 109-110
Antonyms. *See* Opposites.
Apostrophe, in contractions, 27-28, 30, 181
Asking sentences. *See* Questions.
Author, 119-120, 130

be, forms of, 105, 109-110
Body, of letter. *See* Message.
Book reports, 122-129
    giving, in class, 129
    preparing for, 122
    writing, 127-128
Books and stories, 117-130
    author of, 119-120, 130
    kinds of, 118, 121-122, 130
        happened in real life (non-fiction),
            121-123
        make-believe (fiction), 121-123, 125
    order of events in, 126, 145-146
    reports. *See* Book reports.
    special parts (dictionary, table of contents),
        120
    table of contents, 120
    telling when and where story happens
        (setting), 125
    title of, 118-120, 130, 147, 182
    what happens in (plot), 121-122, 124-126
    who is in (characters), 123

Capital letters,
    I, 134
    in proper nouns, 75-82, 119, 149, 176
    in sentences, 41-44, 47-48, 51-52, 149, 177
    in letters, 89-90, 95, 177
    in titles of books, 118, 130, 182
    in titles of names, 76
Categorizing, 166
Characters. *See* Books and stories.
Checking and rewriting, 151, 152, 173, 174
Checking skills (review), 14, 30, 54, 66, 84, 96, 116,
    130, 140, 152, 166, 174
Closing, of letter,
    capitalization of, 89, 177
    comma following, 89-90, 181
    defined, 86, 87, 89

Comma,
    in addresses, 91, 180
    in dates, 82, 89, 180
    in letters, 89, 180-181
Commands,
    defined, 45-46, 50
    finding, 46, 54, 179
    naming part of (subject), 45
    period with, 47-48, 52, 178
    writing, 47-48, 52, 54, 178-179
Comparative form of adjectives, 161
Compositions. *See* Book reports, Informal
    compositions, Writing a description,
    Writing a story.
Compound words, 25-26
Contractions, 27-28, 30, 181
Dates,
    in letters, 86-87
    writing, 82
Declarative sentences. *See* Statements.
Describing words, 153-166
    about actions, 163-164, 166
    how big, 157
    what color, 156, 166
    comparing two things (-er), 161
    comparing three or more things (-est), 162
    finding, 156, 157, 163
    how a thing feels, 158
    how a thing looks, 157, 166
    how many, 155, 166
    how a thing smells, 159
    how a thing sounds, 159, 166
    how a thing tastes, 160, 166
    using, 154, 158-159, 160, 165
Descriptive paragraph. *See* Writing a description.
Dictionary, 183-194
    ABC order in, 56, 60
    finding meanings in, 60
    finding spelling of words in, 62-66
    using, 56, 60-66
Doing words. *See* Verbs.
-ed, verbs ending in, 107-108
Editing. *See* Checking and rewriting.
Ending marks of sentences, 41-44, 47-48, 51-52,
    178-179. *See also* Exclamation point, Period,
    Question mark.
-er, describing words ending in, 161
-est, describing words ending in, 162

Exclamation point, 51-52, 179
Exclamations, 49-52, 179
    defined, 49-50
    exclamation point with, 51-52, 179
    finding, 49-50, 54, 179
    writing, 51-52, 54, 179

Fiction. See Books and stories.
Friendly letters, 93-95

Glossary. See Books and stories.
Greeting, of letter,
    capitalization of, 89, 177
    comma following, 89-90, 180-181
    defined, 86-87, 89

Handbook, 175-182
    using the apostrophe, 181
    using capital letters,
        for first words, 177
        for special words, 176
    using the comma, 180-181
    using ending marks,
        exclamation point, 179
        period, 178
        question mark, 179
    writing titles of books, 182
has, have, had, 106, 111-112
Holidays, writing names of, 79-80
Homographs. See Words.
Homonyms. See Words.

I and me, 133-134, 140
Ideas in sentences, 32-34
Imperative sentences. See Commands.
Informal Compositions, 13, 29, 53, 65, 83, 115,
    139, 165
Interrogative sentences. See Questions.
Interviewing, 11-12
Invitations, 87-88
Irregular verbs. See Verbs.

Jobs, 1-7, 9-14

Letters, 85-96, 177, 180-181
    capitalization in, 89-90, 177
    commas in, 89-91, 180-181
    kinds of, 86
        friendly, 93-95
        invitation, 87-88
        thank-you, 89-90
    parts of, 86-89, 93-96
    writing, 87-90, 93-96

Listening,
    to get specific information, 2, 11-12
    to others, 129
    for rhymes, 17-18
    for sounds in words, 61-64
    to stories, 1, 15, 31, 55, 67, 85, 97, 117, 131, 141,
        153, 167

me and I, 133-134, 140
Message, of letter, 86, 87, 90, 94-95
Modifiers. See Describing words.
Months, writing names of, 81-82

Names, capitalization, 75-76, 84, 176
Naming part of a sentence (subject),
    in commands, 45
    defined, 35
    finding, 35-36, 38, 54, 69, 103-104
    I in, 133-134, 137
    nouns as, 69
    pronouns as, 133-137
    we in, 135-137
Naming words. See Nouns.
Narrative paragraph. See Writing a Story.
Nonfiction. See Books and stories.
Nouns, 67-84
    defined, 68-69
    finding, 68-70, 73, 84
    form changes of (irregular plurals), 74
    in the naming part of a sentence (subject), 69
    in the telling part of a sentence (predicate), 70
    modifiers used to describe, 155
    naming more than one (plural), 71-74, 84
    naming one (singular), 71-74
    proper, 75-82, 84, 149, 176
    pronouns used instead of, 132
    using, 69-70, 83

Opposites (antonyms), 23-24, 30
Oral reports, 11-12, 129

Past forms. See Verbs.
Periods,
    in sentences, 41-42, 47-48, 52, 149, 178
    in titles in names, 76, 178
Plans for writing,
    book reports, 127
    descriptions, 169-170
    stories, 144-150, 152
Plot. See Books and stories.
Plural forms. See Nouns, Verbs.
Poems, 16-18, 195-198 (Teacher's Edition)

Predicate. *See* Telling part of a sentence.
Present forms. *See* Verbs.
Proofreading. *See* Checking and rewriting.
Pronouns, 131-140
    defined, 132
    finding, 132
    I and *me*, 133-134, 140
    in the naming parts of sentences, 133-137
    in other parts of sentences, 133-138
    using, 132-140
    we and *us*, 135-136
Proper nouns, 75-82, 84, 149, 176
    names of days of week, 79, 82, 176
    names of holidays, 79-80, 176
    names of months, 81-82, 176
    names of people and pets, 75, 76, 176
    names of places, 77-78, 176
Punctuation. *See* Comma, Exclamation point, Period,
    Question mark.

Question mark, 43-44, 48, 52, 149, 179
Questions,
    defined, 39-40, 46, 50
    finding, 39-40, 46, 50, 54, 179
    question mark with, 43-44, 48, 52, 149, 179
    writing, 43-44, 48, 52, 54, 179

Reading a description, 171
Regular verbs. *See* Verbs.
Reports. *See* Book reports, Oral reports.
Review. *See* Checking skills.
Revising. *See* Checking and rewriting.
Rhyming words, 17-18, 30

Sentences, 31-54
    capitalization of, 41-44, 47-48, 51-52, 149, 177
    complete idea in, 33-34
    defined, 33-34
    ending marks in, 41-44, 47-48, 51-52, 178-179
    identifying, 32-34
    kinds of,
        commands, 45-48, 50, 52, 54
        exclamations, 49-52, 54
        questions, 39-40, 46, 48, 50, 52, 54
        statements, 39-42, 46, 48, 50, 52, 54
    naming part of (subject), 35-36, 38, 54,
        69, 103-104, 133, 135, 137
    punctuation of. *See* Sentences, ending
        marks in.
    telling part of (predicate), 37-38, 54, 70, 98-101
        word order in, 32-33
Setting of story. *See* Books and stories.

Singular forms. *See* Nouns, Verbs.
Speaking, 1-14
    about books, 129
    about jobs, 1-7, 10-13
    to get or give help, 7-10, 14
    interviewing, 11-12
    to share information, 9-11
    on the telephone, 7-8, 14
Special names. *See* Nouns, proper.
Statements,
    defined, 39-40, 46, 50
    finding, 39-40, 46, 50, 54, 179
    period with, 41-42, 48, 52, 149, 179
    writing, 41-42, 48, 52, 54, 178-179
Stories, to be read to students,
    Anatole and the Cat, by Eve Titus, 196
    Busy Day, Busy People, by Tibor Gergely, 195
    City ABC's, by Michael Deasy, 196
    A Day at the Beach, by Mircea Vasiliu, 195
    Fiona's Bee, by Beverly Keller, 197
    If You Were an Ant, by Barbara Brenner, 198
    Jasper and the Hero Business, by Betty
        Horvath, 197
    Maila and the Flying Carpet, by Denise and
        Alain Trez, 197
    Mike Mulligan and His Steam Shovel, by
        Virginia Lee Burton, 196
    My Sister and I, by Helen E. Buckley, 195
    Sally's Caterpillar, by Anne Rockwell, 198
    Stone Soup, by Marcia Brown, 195
Stories, reading. *See* Books and stories.
Stories, writing. *See* Writing a story.
Subject. *See* Naming part of a sentence.
Superlative form of adjectives, 162
Synonyms. *See* Words

Table of contents, 120
Telephone, using the, 7-8, 14
Telling part of a sentence (predicate),
    defined, 37
    finding, 37-38, 54, 70, 99-101
    nouns in, 70
    verbs in, 98-101
Telling sentences. *See* Statements.
Thank-you letters, 89-90
Titles,
    of books and stories, 118-120, 130, 147, 182
    of persons, 76, 178

Underlining of book titles, 118, 182
Understood subjects of commands. *See you.*
us and *we*, 135-136

201

Verbs, 97-116
  be, 105, 109-110
  defined, 99-101
  -ed ending to show past (regular), 107-108
  finding, 99-103, 107-109, 111, 113, 116
  have, 106, 111-112
  past forms, 107-114, 116
  s ending to show number, 103-104
  that tell about more than one (plural), 103-106
  that tell about one (singular), 103-106
  that add *-ed* to tell about the past (regular), 107-108
  that change in special ways to tell about past (irregular), 109-114
  that tell what happens now (present), 107-114, 116
Vocabulary development. *See* Describing words, Words.

was, were, 109-110
we and *us,* 135-136
Words, 15-30
  ABC order of, 56-60, 66
  compound, 25-26
  contractions, 27-28, 30, 181
  describing. *See* Describing words.
  in dictionary, 56, 60, 62-66
  finding the meaning of, 60
  finding the spelling of, 62-66
  having almost the same meanings (synonyms), 21-22, 30
  having different meanings but sounding the same (homonyms), 19
  having different meanings but spelled the same (homographs), 16, 20
  having opposite meanings (antonyms), 23-24, 30
  listening for sounds in, 61-64
  order of, in sentences, 32-33
  rhyming, 17-18, 30
Writing book reports. *See* Book reports.
Writing a description, 167-174
  checking and rewriting, 173-174
  choosing a plan for, 169-170, 172
  description defined, 168
  steps for, 172
  using describing words, 172
Writing letters. *See* Letters.
Writing a story, 141-152
  beginning sentence, 148, 152
  checking and rewriting, 151
  choosing a title, 147
  ending sentence, 150
  identifying ideas that belong together, 143-144
  making a plan for, 144-150, 152
  ordering ideas for, 145-146, 152
  rules for, 149
  See also Informal compositions, Letters, Writing a description, Writing letters.

you, used as naming part of command (understood subject), 45

ZIP code, 91-92

Acknowledgments (continued) Four Winds Press, A Division of Scholastic Magazines, Inc.: For an excerpt from *Sally's Caterpillar* by Anne Rockwell; copyright © 1966 by Anne Rockwell. Harper & Row, Publishers, Inc.: For an excerpt from *If You Were an Ant* by Barbara Brenner; text copyright © 1973 by Barbara Brenner. Houghton Mifflin Company: For an excerpt from *Mike Mulligan and His Steam Shovel* by Virginia Lee Burton, published by Houghton Mifflin Company; copyright 1939 and © renewed 1967 by Virginia Lee Demetrios. Lothrop, Lee & Shepard Co., Inc.: For stanzas abridged from *My Sister and I* by Helen E. Buckley; copyright © 1963 by Lothrop, Lee & Shepard Co., Inc. (A Division of William Morrow & Co.). McGraw-Hill Book Company: For a selection from *Anatole and the Cat* by Eve Titus, used by permission of the author; copyright © 1957 by Eve Titus. Random House, Inc.: For an excerpt from *Busy Day, Busy People* by Tibor Gergely; copyright © 1973 by Random House, Inc. For an excerpt from *A Day at the Beach* by Mircea Vasiliu; copyright © 1978 by Random House. Charles Scribner's Sons: For a condensed version of *Stone Soup* by Marcia Brown; copyright 1947 by Marcia Brown. For the cover of *Hawk, I'm Your Brother* by Byrd Baylor and illustrated by Peter Parnall; text copyright © 1976 by Byrd Baylor, illustration copyright © 1976 by Peter Parnall. Viking Penguin Inc.: For an excerpt from *Maila and the Flying Carpet* by Denise and Alain Trez; copyright © 1969 by Denise and Alain Trez. Walker and Company, Inc.: For an excerpt from the book, *City ABC's* by Michael Deasy; text copyright © 1974 by Michael Deasy. Franklin Watts, Inc.: For a selection from *Jasper and the Hero Business* by Betty Horvath; copyright © 1977 by Franklin Watts. Albert Whitman & Company: For the cover of *What Mary Jo Wanted* by Janice May Udry, illustration © 1968 by Eleanor Mill.

Photographs
Cover   Photo Researchers: Jerry Cooke.   Other photographs   James L. Ballard.

Illustrations Marc Brown: 1, 7, 14, 39, 45, 104, 108; Kinuko Craft: 3, 4, 10, 19, 31, 70, 159, 161; Gwen Connelly: 5, 8, 23, 25, 32, 88, 133; Karen Ackoff: 6, 7, 10, 13, 20, 37, 69, 129, 149, 153; Larry Fredericks: 6, 7, 9, 10, 13, 47, 48, 107, 113, 114, 147, 148, 150; Kenneth Izzi: 6, 8, 11, 12, 173; Lynn Sweat: 6, 7, 10, 13, 89, 98, 110, 111, 112, 156, 172; James Watling: 6, 7, 10, 13, 55, 59, 67, 68, 137, 143, 146; Monica Santa: 15, 22, 71, 72, 125, 169, 170; Jack Reilly: 16, 18, 24, 34, 44, 56, 58, 61, 81, 101, 109, 118, 161, 162; Carolyn McHenry: 17, 41, 53, 75, 103, 122; Jared Lee: 21, 36, 40, 43, 46, 83, 85, 86, 87, 97, 99, 102, 115, 116, 139; Leslie Robin: 26, 124, 134, 145, 158, 162; Marie De John: 27, 57, 94, 100, 131, 135, 136; Penny Carter: 28, 34, 42, 64, 65, 76, 165; Krystyna Stasiak: 29, 141, 142, 155, 157; Pam Ford-Johnson: 33, 38, 49, 51, 106, 138; Joel Snyder: 52, 60, 132; Dev Appleyard: 62, 77, 78, 121; Howard Berelson: 73, 74, 105; Linda Gist: 164; Jean Helmer: 167, 168, 171; Rodica Prato: 183-194. Handwriting: Robert Smeltzer.